*LOVE is a warm and wonderful
encounter with Leo Buscaglia.
LOVE is a small book
about the largest experience in
the life of a human being.
With all we know, we know
very little about love.
Read this book and learn.*

D0035094

About the author:

Leo Buscaglia is a person who truly
lives as he speaks, who feels and is not
fearful of displaying his emotions, who
loves and is joyous in that love.

A professor of education at the University of Southern California, a native
Californian, an inexhaustible traveler, a
much-loved and carefully-listened-to
speaker, Dr. Buscaglia shares here his
beliefs with us in LOVE.

LOVE

LEO BUSCAGLIA

FAWCETT CREST • NEW YORK

A Fawcett Crest Book
Published by Ballantine Books
Copyright © 1972 by Charles B. Slack, Inc.

ISBN 0-449-20024-8

This edition published by arrangement with
Charles B. Slack, Inc.

Manufactured in the United States of America

First Fawcett Crest Edition: February 1978
First Ballantine Books Edition: May 1982
Third Printing: June 1982

This book is dedicated to Tulio and Rosa Buscaglia, my father and mother who were my best teachers of love, because they never taught me, they showed me.

This book is also dedicated to all those who have helped me to continue to grow in love, and those who will help me tomorrow.

—Leo F. Buscaglia

Contents

"To cheat oneself out of love is the most terrible deception; it is an eternal loss for which there is no reparation, either in time or in eternity."
—*Kierkegaard.*

INTRODUCTION

In the winter of 1969, an intelligent, sensitive female student of mine committed suicide. She was from a seemingly fine upper middle class family. Her grades were excellent. She was popular and sought after. On the particular day in January she drove her car along the cliffs of Pacific Palisades in Los Angeles, left the motor running, walked to the edge of a deep cliff overlooking the sea and leaped to her death on the rocks below. She left no note, not a word of explanation. She was only twenty.

I have never been able to forget her eyes; alert,

alive, responsive, full of promise. I can even recall her papers and examinations which I always read with interest. I wrote on one of her papers which she never received, "A very fine paper. Perceptive, intelligent and sensitive. It indicates your ability to apply what you have learned to your 'real' life. Nice work!" What did I know about her "real" life?

I often wonder what I would read in her eyes or her papers if I could see them now. But, as with so many people and situations in our life, we superficially experience them, they pass and can never again be experienced in the same manner.

I was not blaming myself for her death. I simply wondered what I might have done; if I could have, even momentarily, helped.

It was this question, more than anything else, that led me, in that year, to start an experimental class. It was to be an informal group with voluntary attendance, where any student could be present or drop out at any time, if he so desired. It was to be dedicated to personal growth. I did not want it to become problem-centered or group psychotherapy nor an encounter group. I was an educator, not a psychotherapist. I wanted this class to be a unique experience in learning. I wanted it to have a definite, yet loose, framework and be of broad interest and import to the student. I wanted it to be related to his immediate experience. Students with whom I was relating were, more than ever, concerned with life, living, sex, growth, responsibility, death, hope, the future. It was obvious that the only subject which encompassed, and was at the core of all these concerns and more, was love.

I called the class, "Love Class."

I knew beforehand that I could not "teach" — in the formal sense — such a class. It would be presumptuous. I too was limited in my knowledge and experience of the subject. I was as actively engaged as any of my students in discovering what the real meanings of the word were. I would only be able to act as a facilitator to the students as we guided each other closer to an understanding of the delicate phenomenon of human love.

My determination to start such a class was met with no resistance as long as it was taught free of salary and on my own time without load credit. Of course, a few eyebrows were raised by those who didn't consider love a scholarly subject nor a serious part of a university curriculum.

I was highly amused in the ensuing weeks by the odd looks I received from some colleagues. One professor, in discussing my plans over lunch in the Faculty Center, called love—and anyone who purported to teach it — "irrelevant!" Others asked mockingly and with a wild leer, if the class had a lab requirement and was I going to be the primary investigator.

Nevertheless, student attendance at the class kept

growing until we had to close enrollment with 100 students per year. The students were of all ages, from freshmen to graduates, obviously of varying degrees of experience and sophistication. All were unique and, as such, had individual approaches to the subject and some special knowledge to share.

This book is an outgrowth of "Love Class." It is, as such, in no way intended to be a scholarly, deeply philosophical or definitive work on love. It's rather a sharing of some of the practical and vital ideas, feelings and observations which emerged from the group that seemed to me relevant to the human condition. It might be said that the classes and I wrote this book together. The book may be said to have over 400 authors.

We never attempted nor in three years were able to define love. We felt as we grew in love, that to define it would be to delimit it and love seemed infinite. As one student stated, "I find love much like a mirror. When I love another, he becomes my mirror and I become his, and reflecting in each other's love we see infinity!"

FORWARD TO LOVE

(An excerpt from a speech delivered in Texas 1970—and since.)

If we are going to be "loving" together, it's important that you know who I am and where I'm "at." My name is B-U-S-C-A-G-L-I-A, and it's pronounced like everything in the world. I always start by telling this story because I think it's delightful. Recently I placed a long distance call, the line was busy, and the operator said she'd call me back. I gave her my name, waited a while, and then the phone rang. When I picked it up, she said, "Would you please tell Dr. Boxcar that his telephone call is through?" I said, "Could that be Buscaglia?" She giggled and said, "Sir, it could be damn near anything!"

I have a wonderful time with my name because not only is it Buscaglia, but if you'll look at it you'll see that it's also Leo F. Well, it's really Leonardo, the middle initial is F., but that's really the first name, and it's Felice, that means happiness. Isn't that fantastic? Felice Leonardo Buscaglia! Recently I wanted to visit the Communist-block countries, and I needed a visa. I was in a large room in Los Angeles and filled out a very official form which I turned in. After which, I was asked to sit down and wait for my name to be called. When the time came, this poor man stood at his counter for a moment and looked at the form and I knew it was me he was going to call. He did sort of a double take, took a deep breath, looked up, and said, "Phyllis?" And I swear I'll answer to anything, but Phyllis.

Yes, I am in a "love bag," and I'm not ashamed of it. I have one single message, and I can give you that now. Then you can lay the book aside, go for a walk and hold hands with someone or what you will.

We are in a time in our society when we're really beginning to look at what life is all about, what is learning, and what are the processes of change. We're becoming acquainted with a new nomencla-

ture. We're looking at "conditioning," we're looking at "behavior shaping and modification,"
reinforcement, that it is necessary to reinforce, that
what is reinforced will probably affect behavior.
We are using all kinds of things to reinforce. We're
using money, we're using bells, we're using electric
shocks. We're even using candy. M & M's have become the big thing, and when somebody gives the
correct response, we pop an M & M into his mouth.
My message to you today is simply that the best
M & M in the world is a warm, pulsating, non-
melting human being — YOU! Real love is a very
human phenomenon.

About five years ago I started a love class at the
University. I am — I'm teaching a class in love, and
we are probably the only University in the country
that does have such a class. It meets on Tuesday
nights. We sit on the floor and relate, and I'm sure
the vibrations are felt all over the world. I don't
teach love, of course, I simply facilitate growth in
love.

Love is a learned phenomenon, and I think the
sociologists, the anthropologists, the psychologists,
will tell us this with no hesitation. What worries me
is that maybe many of us are not happy with the
way we've learned it. As experienced human beings
we must certainly believe in one thing more than
anything else — we believe in change. And so, if you
don't like where you're at in terms of love, you can

change it, you can create a new scene. You can only give away what you have. That's the miracle. If you have love, you can give it. If you don't have it, you don't have it to give. Actually it's not really even a matter of giving, is it? It's a matter of sharing. Whatever I have I can share with you. I don't lose it because I still have it. For example, I could teach every reader everything I know. I would still know everything I know. It is possible for me—and not unreasonable — to love everyone with equal intensity and still have all the love energy I have ever had. There are a lot of miracles to being a human being, but this is one of the greatest miracles.

Only recently has it become at all defensible to even mention the word "love." Every time I go to speak somewhere, someone asks, "Will you talk about love?" I reply, "Sure," and they say, "What's your title?" I reply, "Let's just call it 'Love.'" There's a brief hesitation, and then they say, "Well, you know, this is a professional meeting, and it may not be understood. What will the press say?" So I suggest "Affect as a Behavior Modifier," and they agree that sounds more acceptable and scientific, and everyone is happy.

Love has really been ignored by the scientists. It's amazing. My students and I did a study. We went through books in psychology. We went through books in sociology. We went through books in anthropology, and we were hardpressed to find even a reference to the word "love." This is shocking because it is something we all know we need, something we're all continually looking for, and yet there's no class in it. It's just assumed that it comes to us by and through some mysterious life force.

One of Pitirim Sorokin's last books was called *The Ways and Power of Love*. It's full of wonderful studies of affect in which this man engaged because he was really worried about the fact that everybody seemed to be going in opposite directions. Dr. Albert Schweitzer said, "We are all so much together, but we are all dying of loneliness." I feel this, you know this, and Dr. Sorokin thought it was true, too. In his book he is trying to share some of the things that might bring us together again. If we've ever needed it, we need it now. In his book's introduction, he says this: "The sensate mind emphatically disbelieves in the power of love. It appears to us something illusionary. We call it self-deception, the opiate of the people's mind, unscientific bosh and unscientific delusion." Some of you were brought up in Econ I class with a textbook by Samuelson. Remember that dreary book? Yet in his latest edition after five editions — can you imagine five editions of the same book? — there is a chapter that's going to freak you, called "Love and Economics." It's a beautiful chapter. In his introduction, he says, "I know my colleagues at Harvard are going to say I have lost my mind, but I want them to know that I have just found it."

Sorokin also says, "We are biased against all theories that try to prove the power of love in determining human behavior and personality, in influencing the course of biological, social, mental and moral evolution, in affecting the direction of historical events and in shaping social institutions and culture. In the sensate milieu they appear to be unconvincing, certainly unscientific, prejudiced, and superstitious." And I think that's really where we are. Love is prejudicial, superstitious, unscientific bosh.

I'd like to relate with you about some of the ways in which I think we can be reinforcing, non-melting, gorgeous, tender, loving human persons. First of all the loving individual has to care about himself. This is number one. I don't mean an ego trip. I'm talking about somebody who really cares about himself, who says, "Everything is filtered through me, and so the greater I am, the more I have to give. The greater knowledge I have, the more I'm going to have to give. The greater understanding I have, the greater is my ability to teach others and to make myself the most fantastic, the most beautiful, the most wondrous, the most tender human being in the world."

Some exciting work has been going on in California by some great humanist psychologists like

Rogers, Maslow, and Herbert Otto. These men and others are saying that only a small portion of what we are, are we, and that there is an enormous potential in the human being, that it isn't outlandish to say that if we really desired to fly, we could fly! We could have the ability to feel that would be so spectacular that we could feel color! We could have the ability to see better than an eagle, the ability to smell better than a birddog, and a mind that could be so big, it would constantly be full of exciting dreams. Yet we are perfectly happy to be only a small portion of what we are. A London psychiatrist, R.D. Laing, in his book, *The Politics of Experience*, suggests something very provoking — something alien and rather frightening, yet a wondrous challenge. He says, "What we think is less than what we know: What we know is less than what we love: What we love is so much less than what there is; and to this precise extent, we are much less than what we are." Isn't that a mind blower?

Knowing this, we should have a tremendous desire to become. If all of life is directed toward the process of becoming, of growing, of seeing, of feeling, of touching, of smelling, there won't be a boring second. I scream at my students, "Think of what you are and all the fantastic potential of you."

It seems to me that in the past we have not sufficiently celebrated the wonderful uniqueness of every individual. I would agree that personality is the sum total of all the experiences that we have known since the moment of conception to this point in our life along with heredity. But what is often ignored is an X factor. Something within the *you* of *you* that is different from every single human being, that will determine how you will project in this world, how you will see this world, how you will become a special human being. That uniqueness is what worries me because it seems to me that we're dropping it; we're losing it. We're not stressing it; we're not persuading people to discover it and develop it.

Education should be the process of helping everyone to discover his uniqueness, to teach him how to develop that uniqueness, and then to show him how to share it because that's the only reason for having anything. Imagine what this world would be like if all along the way you had people say to you, "It's good that you're unique; it's good that you're different. Show me your differences so that maybe I can learn from them." But we still see the processes again and again of trying to make everyone like everybody else.

A few years ago with some of my student teachers at the University, I went back into classrooms and was astounded to find the same things going on that had been going on when I was in school — a million years ago. For example, the art teacher would come in. Remember how we always anticipated and got

ready for the art teacher? You put your papers
down and you got your Crayolas out and you
waited and finally in would walk this harried person. I really feel sorry for an itinerant art teacher.
She comes racing in from another class and has time
only to nod to the teacher, turn around and say,
"Boys and girls, today we are going to draw a tree."
She goes to the blackboard, and she draws *her* tree
which is a great big green ball with a little brown
base. Remember those lollipop trees? I never saw a
tree that looked like that in my life, but she puts it
up there, and she says, "All right, boys and girls,
draw." Everybody gets busy and draws.

If you have any sense, even at that early age, you
realize that what she really wanted was for you to
draw *her* tree, because the closer you got to her
tree, the better your grade. If you already realized
this in grade one, then you handed in a little lollipop, and she said, "Oh, that's divine." But here's
Junior who really knows a tree as this little woman
has never seen a tree in her life. He's climbed a tree,
he's hugged a tree, he's fallen out of a tree, he's
listened to the breeze blow through the branches.
He really knows a tree, and he knows that a tree
isn't a lollipop! So he takes purple and yellow and
orange and green and magenta crayons and he
draws this beautiful freaky thing and hands it in.
She takes one look and shrieks, "Brain damaged!"

There's a wonderful story in education that always amuses me. It's called *The Animal School*. I always love to tell it because it's so wild, yet it's true. Educators have been laughing at it for years, but nobody does anything about it. The animals got together in the forest one day and decided to start a school. There was a rabbit, a bird, a squirrel, a fish and an eel, and they formed a Board of Education. The rabbit insisted that running be in the curriculum. The bird insisted that flying be in the curriculum. The fish insisted that swimming be in the curriculum, and the squirrel insisted that perpendicular tree climbing be in the curriculum. They put all of these things together and wrote a Curriculum Guide. Then they insisted that *all* of the animals take *all* of the subjects. Although the rabbit was getting an A in running, perpendicular tree climbing was a real problem for him; he kept falling over backwards. Pretty soon he got to be sort of brain damaged, and he couldn't run any more. He found that instead of making an A in running, he was making a C and, of course, he always made an F in perpendicular climbing. The bird was really beautiful at flying, but when it came to burrowing in the ground, he couldn't do so well. He kept breaking his beak and wings. Pretty soon he was making a C in flying as well as an F in burrowing, and he had a hellava time with perpendicular tree climbing. The moral of the story is that the person who was valedictorian of the class was a mentally retarded eel who did everything in a half-way fashion. But the educators were all happy because everybody was taking all of the subjects, and it was called a broad-based education. We laugh at this, but that's what it is. It's what you did. We really are trying to make everybody the same as everybody else, and one soon learns that the ability to conform governs success in the educational scene.

Conformity continues right on into the university. We in higher education are as guilty as everyone else. We don't say to people, "Fly! Think for your-selves." We give them our old knowledge, and we say to them, "Now this is what is essential. This is what is important." I know professors who teach nothing but one best "way," they don't say, "Here are a lot of tools, now go create you own. Go into abstract thinking. Go into dreaming. Dream a while. Find something new." Could it not be that among their students there are greater dreamers than them-selves? So, it all starts with you. You can only give what you have to give. Don't give up your tree. Hold onto your tree. You are the only you — the only magical combination of forces that will be and ever has been that can create such a tree. You are the best you. You will always be the second best anyone else.

We are living in a culture where a person is not measured by who he is or what he is but rather by what he has. If he has a lot, he must be a great man.

LOVE

If he has little, he must be insignificant. About seven years ago I decided that I was going to do something really weird, at least at that time it was considered weird. I was going to sell everything I had, my car, my life insurance policy, my house, all the "important" things, and I was going to take off for a couple of years. I was going to look for *me*. I spent most of my time in Asia because I knew less about Asia than any other part of the world. The countries of Asia are underdeveloped countries. They have very little and, therefore, they must be terribly insignificant. Well, I found out very differently. Those of you who have been there or have delved into Asian culture will agree how wrong this Western concept is. I learned many, many things in Asia that I brought back with me which have really put me on a different path. Where it is leading I don't know and I don't care, but it's different and exciting and wondrous.

I found a very interesting thing in Cambodia. The country is made up mostly of a great lake called the Tonle Sap. Many people live and work around it. When tourists go to Cambodia, they go directly to Angkor Wat, as they should; it's fantastic. The Buddhist ruins being devoured by forests of great trees with monkeys swinging through them are unbelievable. It's beyond your wildest dreams. While I was there, I met a French woman who loved the country so much she stayed on after the French left Cambodia, even though she was a secondary citizen. She really loved the people and the country, and she was willing to put up with whatever it meant. She said to me, "You know, Leo, if you really want to find these people, you won't find them in the ruins. You'll find them in their villages. Take my bicycle and go to the Tonle Sap and see what's happening now."

Nature in Cambodia is very severe. Every year the monsoons come and wash everything into the rivers and streams and lakes. So you don't build great permanent mansions because nature has told you that it will only be washed away. You build little huts. Tourists look and say, "Aren't they quaint but poor people! living in such squalor." It's not squalor. It's how you perceive it. They love their houses which are comfortable and exactly right for their climate and culture. So I went to the lake. I found the people in the process of getting together and preparing for the monsoons. This meant that they were constructing big communal rafts. When the monsoons come and wash away their houses, several families get on a raft and live together about six months of the year. Wouldn't it be beautiful to live with your neighbors? Just think if we could make a raft together and live together for six months of the year! What would probably happen to us? All of a sudden we would again realize how important it is to have a neighbor — that I need you because today you may catch the fish that we will eat or I like you because I can sit down and talk with you if I'm lonely and learn from you and understand another world. After the rains are over, the families once again live as independent units.

I wanted to help them move so I walked in and offered myself in sign language. But they had nothing to move. A few pots and pans, a couple of mats, a few articles of clothing. I thought, "What would you do if tomorrow there were a monsoon in Los Angeles? What would you take? Your TV set? Your automobile? The vase that Aunt Catherine brought from Rome?" Think about that. This was dramatically portrayed to us during the Los Angeles fires. A couple of pictures appeared in the *Los Angeles Times* that really freaked me. One was of a woman running down the streets of Malibu with a great pile of books, her house in the background being consumed by flames. I thought, "Wow, I would like to know this woman. I would like to know what are those books that she considered to be so valuable." I brought the picture to a graduate seminar of supposedly really beautiful students. I asked, "What do you think those books were?" You know what they said? "Her income tax reports!" That's where we are in the U.S.A. I even heard of one woman who fled with her blue chip stamps! She said, "I don't know why I did it," which shows you how silly it all is. But you know what she did have?

She still had herself! That's what it's all about. In the end, you have only you.

Then I think this loving person rids himself of labels. You know, we are really marvelous. Being human is the greatest thing in the world, but we're also funny, and we have to learn to laugh again. After all, we do funny things. We created time, for instance, and then became the slave of time. Like now — you may be thinking in the back of your mind that you have only ten minutes before you must do this or that. You may be somewhere where something really incredible is happening, but it's 10:07, time to leave, and so you've got to move on. We have bells which ring. Bells! Everytime we hear a bell, we respond. It tells us that we must be here or we must be there. We created time, and now we have become the slave of time.

The same thing is true with words. When you read books like Hayakawa's *The Use and Misuse of Language* or Wendell Johnson's book, *People in Quandaries*, you see how tremendously powerful language is. A word is just a few phonetic meaningless symbols side by side. You give it meaning, and then it sticks with you. You give it a cognitive meaning, and you give it an emotional meaning, and then you live with it. Dr. Timothy Leary did some fantastic work on the mind when he was at Harvard. He said, "Words are a freezing of reality." Once you learn a word and get the intellectual and

27

emotional meaning of that word, you are stuck with that word the rest of your life. So, your world of words is built. Everything that happens is filtered through this stuck, frozen system, and that keeps us from growing. We say things like "He's a Communist." Pow! we turn him off. We stop listening. Some people say, "He's a Jew." Pow! we turn him off. We've ceased respecting him. "He's a Dago." Pow! Labels, labels, labels! How many kids have not been educated just because someone pinned a label on them somewhere along the line? Stupid, dumb, emotionally disturbed. I have never known a stupid child. Never! Never! I've only known children and never two alike. Labels are distancing phenomena. They push us away from each other. Black men. What's a black man? I've never known two alike. Does he love? Does he care? What about his kids? Has he cried? Is he lonely? Is he beautiful? Is he happy? Is he giving something to someone? These are the important things. Not the fact that he is a black man or Jew or Dago or Communist or Democrat or Republican.

I had a very unique experience in my childhood. You can look in the annals because it's all recorded. I was born in Los Angeles, and my parents were Italian immigrants. A big family. Mama and Papa were obviously great lovers! They came from a tiny village at the base of the Italian Swiss Alps where everyone knew everyone. Everyone knew the names of the dogs, and the village priest came out and danced in the streets at the fiestas and got as drunk as everybody else. It was the most beautiful scene in the world and a pleasure to be raised by these people in this old way. But when I was taken, at five, to a public school, tested by some very official-looking person, the next thing I knew I was in a class for the mentally retarded! It didn't matter that I was able to speak Italian and an Italian dialect. I also spoke some French and Spanish — but I didn't speak English too well and so I was mentally retarded. I think the term now is "culturally disadvantaged." I was put into this class for the mentally retarded, and I never had a more exciting educational experience in my life! Talk about a warm, pulsating, loving teacher. Her name was Miss Hunt, and I'm sure she was the only one in the school who would teach those "dumb" kids. She was a great bulbous woman. She liked me even if I smelled of garlic. I remember when she used to come and lean over me, how I used to cuddle! I did all kinds of learning for this woman because I really loved her. Then one day I made a tremendous mistake. I wrote a newspaper as if I were a Roman. I described how the gladiators would perform and so on. The next thing I knew I was being retested and was transferred to a regular classroom after which I was bored for the rest of my educational career.

This was a traumatic time for me. People went

around calling me a Dago and a Wop, very popular expressions at that time. I didn't understand it. I remember talking to Papa, who was a big—still is—patriarchal type of guy. I asked, "What is a Dago? What is a Wop?" And he replied, "Oh, never mind, Felice, people always call names. It doesn't mean anything. They don't know anything about you by calling you names. Don't let it bother you." But it did! It did because it distanced me. It put me aside. It gave me a label. I felt a little sorry, too, because it meant that these people didn't know anything about me, although they thought they did, by calling me a Dago. That categorized me. That made them comfortable. They didn't know, for instance, that my mother was a singer and that my dad was a waiter when he first came to this country. He used to work most of the night, and Mama was a little bit lonely. And so she would gather all eleven of us around and play *Aida* or *La Boheme*, how we'd fight over the roles! I remember I was the best Butterfly in the family. I still am, and when the Metropolitan Opera discovers me, they'll have their definitive performance. By the time we were ten or eleven, we knew these operas by heart and could play all the roles. People missed all this by a narrow label.

They also didn't know, for instance, that Mama thought that no diseases would come if you had garlic around your neck. She'd rub garlic and tie it up in a hanky and put it around our necks and send us off to school. And I'll tell you a small secret: I had perfect health. I was never sick a day. I have my theories about this — I don't think anyone ever got close enough to me to pass any germs. Now, having become sophisticated and having given up my garlic, I get a cold a year. They didn't know this by calling me a Wop and a Dago. And they didn't know about Papa's rule that before we left the table, we had to tell him something new that we had learned that day. We thought this was really horrible — what a crazy thing to do! While my sisters and I were washing our hands and fighting over the soap, I'd say, "Well, we'd better learn something," and we'd dash to the encyclopedia and flip to something like "The population of Iran is one million . . ." and we'd mutter to ourselves "The population of Iran is. . . ." We'd sit down and after a dinner of great big dishes of spaghetti and mounds of veal so high you couldn't even see across the table, Papa would sit back and take out his little black cigar and say, "Felice, what did you learn new today?" And I'd drone, "The population of Iran is. . . ." Nothing was insignificant to this man. He'd turn to my mother and say, "Rosa, did you know that?" She'd reply, impressed, "No." We'd think, "Gee, these people are crazy." But I'll tell you a secret. Even now going to bed at night, as exhausted as I often am, I still lie back and say to myself, "Felice, old boy, what did you learn new today?" And if I can't think of anything, I've got to get a book and flip to something before I can get to sleep. Maybe this is what learning is all about. But they didn't know that when they called me a Dago. Labels are distancing phenomena—stop using them! And when people use them around you, have the gumption and the guts to say, "What and who are you talking about because I don't know any such thing." If each and every one of you stop it, it's going to stop. There is no word vast enough to begin to describe even the simplest of man. But only you can stop it. A loving person won't stand for it. There are too many beautiful things about each human being to call him a name and then put him aside.

Then this loving person must be one who recognizes responsibility. There is no greater responsibility in the world than being a human being, and you'd better believe it.

This loving person is a person who abhors waste —waste of time, waste of human potential. How much time we waste. As if we were going to live forever. I have to tell you this story because it is one of my greatest experiences. We had a young lady in our School of Education that I thought perhaps had the possibilities of being one of the greatest teachers of all time. She was absolutely psychedelic, and she loved kids. She was so turned on that it was impossible to hold her down — "I want to get with them, I want to get with them." She went through school, was graduated and was hired, of course, because she was so beautiful — spiritually, mentally, every way. She was assigned to a first grade class. I remember the whole process because I was let in on it, step by step, in great moments of wonderment on her part.

When she got in her classroom she looked at the Curriculum Guide which said — and you know we are still doing this — the first unit would be "The Store" — the S-T-O-R-E. She looked at it, and she said, "That's not possible. This is 1970, U.S.A. These kids were raised in stores. They were wheeled around in little baskets in stores. They knocked over Campbell Soup cans and they spilled milk. They know what a store is. What are we doing studying a store?" Nevertheless this was what it said in the Curriculum Guide, and so she thought, "Well, maybe there is some merit and I can have a really exciting unit on the store. I'll really try. On that first day she sat down with the kids on the rug, and she said, very enthusiastically, "Boys and girls, how would you like to study the store?" They said, "Rotten!"

Kids are not as stupid nowadays as they used to be. McLuhan has shown that most children have seen 5,000 hours of TV before they reach kindergarten. They have seen murders and rapes, they have seen love affairs, they have heard music, they have been to Paris, to Rome. On their TV set they have seen real people die violently. Then we bring them to school, and we teach them about stores. Or we give them a book that says, "Tom said, 'Oh, Oh.' Mary said 'Oh, Oh.' Grandma said, 'Oh, Oh.' Spot said, 'Oh, Oh.' " Well, damn Spot! It's about time that we started realizing that we are educating *children*, not things. We must say, "Who is the new child we are educating and what are his needs?" How else can he survive tomorrow?

And so this little girl, because she was a real teacher, said, "Okay, what do you want to study?" One little kid's eyes opened real wide, and he said, "You know, my father works at Jet Propulsion Labs, and he can get us a rocket ship, and we could put up a rocket ship and learn all about it and fly to the moon!" All the kids said, "Groovy! That's great!" So she said, "Okay, let's do it." The next day the father came and set up a rocket ship. He sat down on the rug with the kids, and he told them about flying to the moon and how a rocket ship works. You should have seen what was happening in that classroom. They were talking about science astronomy, complex theories of math. They had a vocabulary not of "oh, oh," but of parts of a rocket ship, galaxies, space; a meaningful vocabulary.

Then one day in the middle of all of this fantastic learning, in walked the supervisor. She looked

around and said, "Mrs. W, where is your store?"
Some day I'm going to write this story for *The
New Yorker*, and I'm going to call it "Mrs. W,
Where Is Your Store?" The young teacher took
the supervisor aside, saying, "You know, we talked
about the store, but the kids wanted to fly to the
moon. Look at our vocabulary lists and look at the
books they are making. Next we are going to have
a man from Jet Propulsion who is going to do a
demonstration. . . ." The supervisor said, "Nevertheless, Mrs. W, the Curriculum Guide says you
will have a store, and *you will have a store*"— (tight
smile) —"Won't you, dear?"

She came to me and said, "What's this bit you
have been feeding me about creativity in education,
getting me blown up and excited, and then I begin
teaching, and I have to make clay bananas!" You
ate a banana, you slipped on a banana peel, you got
sick on bananas—then you spent a six-week unit
making artificial clay bananas for the store. Time's
awasting! And so do you know what she did? She
sat down with her kids, and she said, "Kids, do you
want Mrs. W to be here next year?" And they said,
"Oh, yes!" "Well, then, we've got to make a store."
And they said, "Okay, let's do it, but let's do it
fast!" In two days they did a six-week unit. They
made those damn clay bananas, and they pounded
boxes together and put everything in them. She
also told them that when the supervisor came, it

LOVE

would be necessary to show her that they could
function in a store. When the supervisor came, she
was very happy because there was the store, and
the little kids would say, "Would you like to buy
some bananas today?" And as soon as she left, they
flew to the moon! Hypocrisy! And waste, waste,
waste!

It isn't enough to live and learn for today. We
have to dream about what the world is going to be
like in fifty years and educate for a hundred years
hence and a dream world of a thousand years hence.
The world today for the first grader is not going
to be his world in thirty years. Look at how *our*
world has changed. No wonder we are confused
and up tight and anxious — we were not prepared
to deal with the world we are living in. And it's
moving so fast! There isn't time for "Grandma said,
'Oh, Oh.' "

Then I think this loving individual is a person
who is spontaneous. This is something that I feel
really, really strongly about because I think that we
have lost our ability to be spontaneous. We are all
marking time, and we are all regimented. We have
forgotten what it is to laugh and to feel good laughing. We are taught that a young sophisticated lady
does not laugh boisterously — she titters. Who said?
Emily Post? She's sick! Why should we listen to
somebody else tell us how to live our existence?
Yet every day we see in the papers "Dear Miss Post,

My daughter is being married in February. What kind of flowers should she carry?" If your daughter wants to carry radishes, let her carry them. "Dear Interior Decorator, I have puce curtains in my living room. What color should my rug be?" I can just see this little cat sitting in his office saying, "Hey, heh, heh." And he replies, "Purple." So you run out and buy thousands of dollars worth of purple rugs with puce curtains, and you're stuck with them, and you deserve it! We don't trust our own feelings any more. Men don't cry. Who said? If you feel like crying, you cry. I cry all the time. I cry when I'm happy, I cry when I'm sad, I cry when a student says something beautiful, I cry when I read poetry.

If you feel something, let people know that you feel it. Don't you get tired of these stoic faces that don't show anything? If you feel like laughing, laugh. If you like what somebody says, go up and give them a hug. If it is right, it will be right. Spontaneity again, living again, knowing what it is like to tingle. Sometimes I get up in the morning, and I feel so freaky and good, I can't stand it. I remember once driving to work, and I was singing Butterfly, the love duet, both roles, best performance I'd ever given, and a policeman stuck his head in the window, he had a great big grin on his face, and he said, "This is going to be the funniest ticket I've ever given." I said, "How's that, Officer?" He said,

"I was chasing someone for speeding, and you passed us both up." I love that. I hadn't even seen him. I was in my own beautiful world.

We are constantly moving away from ourselves and others. The scene seems to be how far away you can get from another person, not how close you can get to them. I'm all for going back to the old-fashioned thing of touching people. My hand always goes out because when I touch somebody, I know they are alive. We really need that affirmation. The existentialist says that we all think we are invisible and that sometimes we have to commit suicide to affirm the fact that we have lived at all. Well, I don't want to do that. There are better, less drastic ways of affirming it. If somebody hugs you, you know you must be there or they'll go through you. I hug everybody — just come close to me, you're more than likely to get hugged, certainly touched.

We need not be afraid to touch, to feel, to show emotion. The easiest thing in the world to be is what you are, what you feel. The hardest thing to be is what other people want you to be, but that's the scene we are living in. Are you really you or are you what people have told you you are? And are you interested in really knowing who you are because if you are, it is the happiest trip of your life.

And this loving person is also one who sees the continual wonder and joy of being alive. I am sure that contrary to the media, we were meant to be happy because there are so many beautiful things in our world — trees and birds and faces. There are no two things alike and things are always changing. How can we get bored? There has never been the same sunset twice. Look at everybody's face. Each face is different. Everybody has his own beauty. There have never been two flowers alike. Nature abhors sameness. Even two blades of grass are different. The Buddhists taught me a fantastic thing. They believe in the here and the now. They say that the only reality is what is here, what is happening between you and me right now. If you live for tomorrow, which is only a dream, then all you are going to have is an unrealized dream. And the past is no longer real. It has value because it made you what you are now, but that is all the value it has. So don't live in the past. Live now. When you are eating, eat. When you are loving, love. When you are talking with someone, talk. When you are looking at a flower, look. Catch the beauty of the moment!

The loving person has no need to be perfect, only human. The idea of perfection frightens me. We're almost afraid to do anything anymore because we can't do it perfectly. Maslow says there are marvelous peak experiences that we all should be experiencing, like creating a pot in ceramics or painting a picture and putting it over here and saying,

"That's an extension of me." There's another existentialist theory that says, "I must be because I have done something. I have created something—therefore, I am." Yet we don't want to do this because we're afraid it isn't going to be good, it isn't going to be approved of. If you feel like smearing ink on a wall, you do it. Say, "That came out of me, it's my creation, I did it, and it is good." But we're afraid because we want things to be perfect. We want our children to be perfect.

Drawing from personal experiences, I remember my physical education classes in junior and senior high school. If there are any physical education teachers reading this, I hope they hear me loud and clear. I remember the striving for perfection. Physical education should be a place where we all should have an equal opportunity, where our only competition should be with ourselves. If we can't throw a ball, then we learn to throw a ball the best we can. But that wasn't it — they were always rewarding perfection. There were always the big muscular guys standing up there. They were the stars. And there I was — skin and bones with my little bag of garlic around my neck, and shorts that didn't fit and always hung way down my little skinny legs. I'd stand there in line while we were being chosen in games, and I used to die every single day of my life. You remember! We all lined up, and there were the athletes standing there with their big chests out, and they'd say, "I choose you" and "I choose you" and you saw the line dwindling away, and there you were, still standing there. Finally it got down to two people, one other little skinny guy and you. And then they'd say, "Okay, I'll take Buscaglia" or "I'll take the Wop" and you'd step out of line dying because you were not the image of the athlete, you were not the image of perfection they were striving for. I have a student in class who is a gymnast. He almost made the Olympics last year. He has a club foot. In every other way in this world he is as perfect as you can imagine, a body that would be the envy of anyone, a beautiful mind, fantastic crop of hair, sparkling, alert eyes. But he isn't a beautiful boy in his perception — he's a club foot. Somewhere along the line somebody missed the boat, and all he hears when he walks down the street is the clump of a foot even though no one else is aware of it any longer. But if *he* sees it, then that's what he is. So this idea of perfection really turns me off.

But man is always capable of growth and change, and if you don't believe this, you are in the process of dying. Every day you should be seeing the world in a new personal way. The tree outside your house is no longer the same — so *look* at it! Your husband, wife, child, mother, father all are changing daily so *look* at them. Everything is in the process of change, including you. The other day I was on a beach with some of my students, and one of them picked up an old, dried-out starfish, and with great care he put it back in the water. He said, "Oh, it's just dried out but when it gets moisture again, it's going to come back to life." And then he thought for a minute, and he turned to me, and he said, "You know, maybe that's the whole process of becoming, maybe we get to the point from time to time where we sort of dry out, and all we need is a little more moisture to get us started again." Maybe this is what it's all about.

In fact, an investment in life is an investment in change to the end, and we can't be concerned with dying because we must be too damned busy living! Let dying take care of itself. And don't ever believe that your life is ever going to be peaceful — life is not like that. With change taking place all around you, you've got to continue adjusting which means that you are going to constantly be becoming, there is no stopping. We're all on a fantastic journey! Every day is new. Every experience is new. Every person is new. Everything is new, every morning of your life. Stop seeing it as a drag! In Japan, the running of water is a ceremony. We used to sit in a little hut when the tea ceremony took place, and our host would pick up a scoop of water and pour it into the teapot, and everybody would listen. The sound of the falling water would be almost overpoweringly exciting. I think of how many people run showers and water in their sinks every single day and have never heard it. When was the last time you listened to rain drops?

Herbert Otto says, "Change and growth take place when a person has risked himself and dares to become involved with experimenting with his own life." Isn't that fantastic? A person has risked himself and dared to become involved with experimenting with his own life, trusting himself. To do this, to experiment with your own life, is very exhilarating, full of joy, full of happiness, full of wonder, and yet it's also frightening. Frightening because you are dealing with the unknown, and you are shaking complacency.

I have a very strong feeling that the opposite of love is not hate — it's apathy. It's not giving a damn. If somebody hates me, they must "feel" something about me or they couldn't possibly hate. Therefore, there's some way in which I can get to them. If you don't like the scene you're in, if you're unhappy, if you're lonely, if you don't feel that things are happening, change your scene. Paint a new backdrop. Surround yourself with new actors. Write a new play. And if it's not a good play, get the hell off the stage and write another one. There are millions of plays — as many as there are people. Nikos Kazantzakis says, "You have your brush and colors, paint paradise, and in you go."

A loving person recognizes needs. He needs people who care, someone who cares at least about him, who truly sees and hears him. Again, perhaps just one person but someone who cares deeply. Sometimes it takes only one finger to mend a dike.

I don't know how many of you have ever seen the play *Our Town* but one of its most poignant scenes is when little Emily dies, and she goes into the graveyard, and the gods tell her that she can come back to life for one day. She chooses to go back and relive her twelfth birthday. She comes down the stairs in her birthday dress, her curls bouncing, so happy because she is the birthday girl. And Mama is so busy making a cake *for* her that she doesn't look up to see her. Papa comes in, and he is so busy with his books and his papers and making his money, that he walks right by, doesn't even see her. Her brother is in his own scene, and he's not bothering to look either. Emily finally ends up in the center of the stage alone, in her little birthday dress. She says, "Please, somebody, look at me." She goes to her mother once again, and she says, "Mama, please, just for a minute, look at me." But nobody does, and she turns to the gods, if you remember, and her line is something like, "Take me away. I forgot how difficult it was to be a human being. Nobody looks at anybody anymore."

It's also about time we started listening to each other. We need to be heard. I used to love the idea of "share and tell" in the classroom. I thought this was a time when people would listen. But, you see, someone told the teachers that they had to have their enrollment slips in by 9:05 so they used this time for share and tell. Little kids went up and said, "Last night my daddy hit my mommy with the rolling pin and knocked out two front teeth, and the ambulance came and took her away, and she's in the hospital." And the teacher looked up and said, "All right, who's next?" Or the little kid came up and showed teacher a rock, "I found a rock on the way to school today." She said, "Fine, Johnny, put it on the science table." I wonder what would happen if she picked the rock up and said, "Let me see the rock. Look at that. Kids, look at the color of that rock. Feel it. Who made a rock? Where does a rock come from? What's a rock? What kind of a rock is this?" I can see how everything could stop all day long, and you could just groove on learning about a rock. But "Put it on the science table."

And man needs a feeling of achievement. We all do. We've got to be able to be recognized for doing something well. And somebody's got to point it out to us. Somebody has got to come up occasionally and pat us on the shoulder and say, "Wow! That's good. I really like that." It would be a miracle if we could let people know what was right rather than always pointing out what is wrong.

And then, the lover, to learn and to change and

to become, also needs freedom. Thoreau said a wonderful thing: "Birds never sing in caves.". And neither do people. You've got to be free in order to learn. You've got to have people who are interested in your tree, not the lollipop tree, and you've got to be interested in their tree. "Show me your tree. Show me who you are, and then I'll know where I can begin." But birds never sing in caves. We need to be free to *create*.

I had an incredible experience recently. I talked to a bunch of gifted kids in a California school district. I ranted and raved in my usual fashion, and they sat there just sort of glued — the vibrations between us were incredible. After the morning session, the faculty took me to lunch. When I came back, the kids met me and said, "Oh, Dr. B., a terrible thing has happened. Remember the boy who was sitting right in front of you there?" And I said, "Oh, yes, I'll never forget him, he was so with it." "Well, he's been thrown out of school for two weeks." I said, "Why?" It seems that in my lecture I had been talking about the way that you know something, really know it, is to experience it fully. And I said, "If you really want to know a tree, for instance, you've got to climb in the tree, you've got to feel the tree, sit in the branches, listen to the wind blow through the leaves. Then you'll be able to say, 'I know that tree'." And the boy had said, "Yeh, man, I'll remember that. That's where it's at." So during lunch time, this kid saw a tree and climbed up in it. The boys' vice principal passed by, saw him up there, dragged him down, and kicked him out of school.

I said, "Oh, there must be a mistake; there was a misunderstanding. I'll go talk to the boys' vice principal." I don't know why it is but boys' vice principals are always ex-P.E. teachers. I went to the office where he was sitting with his bulging muscles, and I said, "I'm Dr. Buscaglia." He looked up at me furious. He said, "You're the man who comes onto this campus and tells kids to climb trees? You're a menace!" And I said, "Well, you didn't understand. I think there was a little mis . . ." He shouted, "You're a menace! Telling kids to climb trees! What if they fell out? They're problems enough!" Well, I never got to him, it was impossible, I couldn't deal with him. So I went to the house of this boy who now had two free weeks to climb trees, I sat down with him, and he said, "I think the thing I've learned from this is when to climb trees and when not to do it. I guess I just used bad judgment, didn't I?" He had listened, and he'll have to adjust to this man in the front office — but he's still climbing trees. There are ways to meet the needs of society, and still do your own thing. It's knowing where and when and how.

Everybody has his own way and must be allowed the freedom to pursue it. There are a thousand

paths to loving. Everyone will find his own way if
he listens to himself. Don't let anybody impose their
way on you. There's a wonderful book called
Teachings According to Don Juan written by an
anthropologist named Carlos Castaneda. It's all
about the Yaqui Indians whom he studied. In it
there is a man called Don Juan, who says, "Each
path is only one of a million paths. Therefore, you
must always keep in mind that a path is only a path.
If you feel that you must now follow it, you need
not stay with it under any circumstances. Any path
is only a path. There is no affront to yourself or
others in dropping it if that is what your heart tells
you to do. But your decision to keep on the path or
to leave it must be free of fear and ambition. I warn
you: Look at every path closely and deliberately.
Try it as many times as you think necessary. Then
ask yourself and yourself alone one question. It is
this: Does this path have a heart? All paths are the
same. They lead nowhere. They are paths going
through the brush or into the brush or under the
brush. Does this path have a heart is the only question. If it does, then the path is good. If it doesn't,
it is of no use." If your path is love the goal is un-
important, the process will have heart.

You can only be "real" on your path. The hardest thing in the world is to be something you're not.
By straying from yourself you must get closer and
closer and closer to what you are. You'll find it's

an easy way to be. The easiest thing to be in the world is you. The most difficult thing to be is what other people want you to be. Don't let them put you in that position. Find "you," who you are, be as you are. Then you can live simply. You can use all of the energy that it takes to "hold back the spooks," as Alpert calls it. You won't have any spooks to hold back anymore. You won't be playing games anymore. Clear them all away and say, "Here's me. Take me for what I am with all my frailties, all my stupidity, and so on. And if you can't, leave me be."

Now we are ready to share a trip into love. This trip is not meant to be a path. It's a sharing. Take what is right for you. But first, I'd like to offer a wondrous bit of philosophy. It's written by a man named Zinker, who is at the Gestalt Institute in Cleveland. He wrote this as the end of a paper which he called *On Public Knowledge and Personal Revolution.* He said, "If a man in the street were to pursue his self, what kind of guiding thoughts would he come up with about changing his existence? He would perhaps discover that his brain is not yet dead, that his body is not dried up, and that no matter where he is right now, he is still the creator of his own destiny. He can change this destiny by taking his one decision to change seriously, by fighting his petty resistances against change and fear, by learning more about his mind, by trying out behavior which fills his real need, by carrying out concrete acts rather than conceptualizing about them" — (I feel strongly about that — let's stop talking and start doing) — "by practicing to see and hear and touch and feel as he has never before used these senses, by creating something with his own hands without demanding perfection, by thinking out ways in which he behaves in a self-defeating manner, by listening to the words that he utters to his wife, his kids, and his friends, by listening to himself, by listening to the words and looking into the eyes of those who speak to him, by learning to respect the process of his own creative encounters and by having faith that they will get him somewhere soon. We must remind ourselves, however, that no change takes place without working hard and without getting your hands dirty. There are no formulae and no books to memorize on becoming. I only know this: I exist, I am, I am here, I am becoming, I make my life and no one else makes it for me. I must face my own shortcomings, mistakes, transgressions. No one can suffer my non-being as I do, but tomorrow is another day, and I must decide to leave my bed and live again. And if I fail, I don't have the comfort of blaming you or life or God."

LOVE IS
A LEARNED
PHENOMENON

"*We are all functioning at a small fraction of our capacity to live fully in its total meaning of loving, caring, creating and adventuring. Consequently, the actualizing of our potential can become the most exciting adventure of our lifetime.*"

—*Herbert Otto.*

I.

At the turn of the century a child was found in the forests of a small village in France. The child had been abandoned for dead by his parents. By some miracle he did not die in the forest. He survived, not as a child, even though he was physically a human being, but rather as an animal. He walked on all fours, made his home in a hole in the ground, had no meaningful language above an animal cry, knew no close relationships, cared about no one or no thing except survival.

Cases such as this — that of Kumala, the Indian

Each man lives love in his limited fashion and does not seem to relate the resultant confusion and loneliness to his lack of knowledge about love.

girl, for instance — have been reported from the beginning of time. They have in common the fact that if man is raised as an animal he will behave as an animal, for man "learns" to be human. Just as man learns to be a human being, so he learns to feel as a human being, to love as a human being.

Psychologists, psychiatrists, sociologists, anthropologists and educators have suggested in countless studies and numerous research papers that love is a "learned response, a learned emotion." How man learns to love seems to be directly related to his ability to learn, those in his environment who will teach him, as well as the type, extent and sophistication of his culture. Family structure, courtship practices, marriage laws, sex taboos, for instance, all vary according to where one lives. The mores and folkways involved in love, sex, marriage and the family are different, for instance, in Bali than they are in New York City. In Bali, for instance, the family structure is close; in Manhattan, it is loose and less structured. In Bali, marriage is polygamous; in Manhattan, at least for legal purposes, monagamous.

These facts concerning the effects of learning upon behavior appear self-evident when stated. Yet, they seem to have little, if any, effect upon the majority of people when applied to love. Most of us continue to behave as though love is not learned but lies dormant in each human being and simply awaits some mystical age of awareness to emerge in full bloom. Many wait for this age forever. We seem to refuse to face the obvious fact that most of us spend our lives trying to find love, trying to live in it, and dying without ever truly discovering it.

There are those who will dismiss love as a naive and romantic construct of our culture. Others will wax poetic and tell you that "love is all," "love is the bird call and the glint in a young girl's eyes on a summer night." Some will be dogmatic and tell you emphatically that "God is Love." And some, according to their own unique experience, will tell us, "Love is a strong, emotional attachment to another . . ." etc. In some cases you will find that people have never thought of questioning love, much less defining it, and object violently even to the suggestion that they think about it. To them love is not to be pondered, it is simply to be experienced. It is true that to some degree all of these statements are correct, but to assume that any one is best or all there is to love, is rather simple. So each man lives love in his limited fashion and does not seem to relate the resultant confusion and loneliness to this lack of knowledge about love.

If he desired to know about automobiles, he would, without question, study diligently about automobiles. If his wife desired to be a gourmet cook, she'd certainly study the art of cooking, perhaps even attend a cooking class. Yet, it never seems as obvious to him that if he wants to live in love, he must spend at least as much time as the auto mechanic or the gourmet in studying love. No mechanic or cook would ever believe that by "willing" the knowledge in his field, he'd ever become an expert in it.

In discussing love, it would be well to consider the following premises:

> One cannot give what he does not possess. To give love you must possess love.

> One cannot teach what he does not understand. To teach love you must comprehend love.

> One cannot know what he does not study. To study love you must live in love.

> One cannot appreciate what he does not recognize. To recognize love you must be receptive to love.

> One cannot have doubt about that which he wishes to trust. To trust love you must be convinced of love.

> One cannot admit what he does not yield to. To yield to love you must be vulnerable to love.

> One cannot live what he does not dedicate himself to. To dedicate yourself to love you must be forever growing in love.

LOVE

A human child, newly born, knows nothing of love. He is totally helpless, mostly ignorant, dependent and vulnerable. If left alone, uncared for for any time before he is six or seven years of age, he will most likely die. He will take longer to learn independence than any living creature. And, it seems that, as societies become more complicated and sophisticated, the time before independence is attained is extended to the point to which the individual remains dependent, if not economically, emotionally, until his death.

As the human child grows, the world which surrounds him, the people interacting in his world, will teach him what love means. At first, it may mean that when he is hungry, lonely, in pain or discomfort, he cries out. His cry may bring a response, usually someone who will feed him so he'll no longer feel hunger pains; hold him so he'll no longer feel lonely; remove or eliminate the source of his pain so he'll again feel comfort. These will be the first interactions which will teach him to identify with another being. He is still not able to relate this source of comfort to a human role, like mother, father, servant, female governess, grandmother. It is likely that if a wolf — which has been known to serve this purpose for a child — were to fulfill his basic needs, he would form an attachment of need to the wolf. But it's not yet love, simply a need attachment. No matter. It is this first reaction-interaction, onesided and simple though it may seem, that eventually will lead to the complicated, multi-faceted phenomenon, love.

At this point, the attitude of the object upon whom the child depends and reacts plays an important role. The object, too, has needs. According to his needs, so will he respond to the child. The reinforcement for a mother's rising in the night and caring for the child or doing the thousand different chores required of the 20th century mother, for example, may be simply the feeling of fulfillment in having created life or the smile of the child or the warmth of the child against her body. But, nevertheless, she'll need the reinforcement or she will abandon the child. According to how these acts meet her needs, so she will respond in kind. It has been noted that in mothers of autistic, totally non-responsive infants, the mothers tend to pull away, to hold the child less, fondle and caress him less, and generally respond to him less.

As the child grows, so does his world and so do his attachments. His world of love is still limited, usually to his family; his father, his brothers, his sisters, but mostly his mother. Each family member in his turn will play a role in teaching the child something of love. He will do this by how he handles the child, how he plays or speaks with him, how he reacts to him. Certainly, no family member has ever set out deliberately to "teach" love to a child. Love is an emotion, that is true. But it is also a "response" to an emotion and, therefore, an "active" expression of what is felt. Love is not learned by osmosis. It is actually acted out and acted upon.

In turn, each family member can teach only what he knows of love. The child will more and more act out what he's learning. Those positive elements he expresses which are approved and reinforced according to the family's feelings and beliefs will be adopted as part of his behavior. Those elements of his expressed behavior of which his family disapproves and which are not reinforced, which may even be punished, will not become a part of his behavorial repertory. For example, if the family is a demonstrative group where affection is outwardly expressed, the child will be reinforced by a positive response when he expresses this. The child leaps into his father's arms and plants a kiss on his mouth, full and juicy. The father returns this in kind, joyfully, verbally, tenderly, smilingly, approvingly. He is teaching the child that this outward expression of love is a good one. On the other hand, a child may spontaneously leap upon his father who may be equally loving, but whose expression of love does not include demonstrative acting out of affection. This father may tenderly hold the child away from him and smilingly say, "Big men don't hug and kiss each other." This father has taught his child that it is well to love, but that an outward show of love is not approved in his environment. The French philosopher, Jean-Paul Sartre, has said, "Long before birth, even before we are conceived, our parents have decided who we shall be."

Aside from the immediate family, there are other influences which teach love. The effect of these influences can be strong. One of these is the individual's culture. It is this culture which, in many cases, has taught the family its responses to love. So it will serve to further reinforce the child's actions.

A French child, for example, born and raised in a Chinese society by Chinese parents, will grow up as a Chinese child with the Chinese child's games, his responses, his manners, his reactions, his likes and dislikes, his language, his aspirations and dreams.

On the other hand, this same French child raised in a Chinese culture by French parents will become a French child in a Chinese society — holding on to those aspects of the French culture he is being taught by his parents and adapting them as he grows up in order to live in a Chinese society. He will then develop those French characteristics common to French children, but will have, also, to adjust them to the Chinese culture.

No person can be totally free of cultural pressures and influences. To become a "socially approved" person, one must always give up some of himself. A Robinson Crusoe can be totally free on his island, but he pays for his freedom with isolation. When Friday, a second person, appears, he has a choice. He can either co-habit with him and make him one like himself which would involve changing his habits and participating in a democratic interchange, or he can make Friday his slave. This decision will require little or no change of Crusoe's personality and life except that he keep a continual, forceful, watchful eye on Friday, his slave.

In the fall of 1970, I had an interesting experience in social living. I enjoy fall leaves, the colors, the sound of the leaves as you walk on them. For this reason, I allow them freely to collect on my path and on the walk that runs before my home. They become like a crackling, multi-colored sound carpet under my feet. One day, I was at home with some students and responded to a knock on the front door. It was a group of neighbors who had come to complain about the accumulation of what they saw as a neighborhood "eyesore." They asked if I would clean up the leaves and they also politely offered to do it for me. I quickly agreed to comply with their request, much to the disillusionment of the students who felt that I had "copped out" and should have told them to which layer of Dante's Hell they might go. I explained that we could reach a mutually satisfactory solution if they'd help me to rake the leaves into the baskets. They complied questioningly and begrudgingly, cursing the "hung-up" culture that would infringe upon an individual's rights. The leaves finally collected, I gathered up the baskets and poured the leaves over my living room floor. Now the neighbors would have a more acceptable scene to gaze upon and I would have my wondrous fall color world to crackle beneath my feet to my heart's content. (It was such a simple thing to sweep and vacuum when I so desired.) I had yielded to the culture, for I enjoy and need neighbors, but I also met my own needs. I enjoy and need fall leaves.

It is possible that when we choose to give up one freedom of a lower order, we achieve a freedom of a still higher order. (By sweeping the leaves I still have neighbors who care. A man never knows when he will need a cup of flour.) The culture and society has the power, then, if we choose to be a member of it, to affect our thoughts, limit our choices, mold our behavior, teach us its definition of adjustment and show us what it means by love.

How you learn love, then, will be somewhat determined by the culture in which you grow.

The unique family and the individual's culture may, at times, come into conflict. My parents and family, a large, warm, demonstrative, highly emotional Italian one, with strong personal ties and attachments, taught me an outward expression of love. But going to school and hugging and kissing the children and teachers was soon taught out of

me as immature, effeminate and, to say the least,
disruptive. I can recall the confusion in my mind
when one of my classmates' mothers came to my
home and explained to my confused parents that I
was not a suitable playmate for their children, that
I was too "physical." But it no longer became a
conflict when it was explained, and I was able to
understand, that when I was in our home and
homes like ours there was a correct way of expressing our affection but in other homes it might be different. I was to observe and respond accordingly,
using my own judgment. By this time of course I
was convinced that a handshake or even a warm
smile could never mean as much pleasure for me as
a warm embrace or a tender kiss. (I still believe it's
true.)

The child, so far, is continually at the mercy of
his teachers — the environment in which he lives and
those individuals (human persons) with whom he'll
come into contact. They are responsible for teaching him to love. His parents, of course, will be his
foremost teachers. They will have the strongest
impact upon him and will teach him only the kind
of love they've learned and only to the degree to
which they've learned it. For they, too, have been
at the mercy of their teachers and their culture.
Teachers can only teach what they have learned.
If the love they've learned is immature, confused,
possessive, destructive, exclusive, then that is what

they'll pass on and teach to their young. If, on the other hand, they know a love that is growing, free, mature, they'll teach this to their children. The child cannot resist his teachers. He has little or no power to do so. In order to exist at some level of comfort, he must accept what is offered, often without question. In fact, he has few questions for he has little knowledge and nothing to compare it to. He is spoon-fed his world, handed the tools to meet its requirements and the symbols with which to organize it. He is even taught what things are significant, what sounds to listen for and what they mean, and what is valueless. In other words, he is taught to be a particular type of human lover. To be loved in return, he need but listen, see and respond as others do. It is a simple matter but the cost to his individuality is great.

Language is the main means by which we transfer knowledge, attitudes, prejudices, feelings and those aspects which make personality and culture unique. Language is taught and learned in and through the family and society. Any normal child has the biological, mental and physical equipment to learn any of the world's languages. He can execute, as an infant, all the sounds of the Universal Phonetic Alphabet. Although he will never be formally taught, by the time he is three or four years of age, he will be speaking, intelligibly, the language of his culture. He'll learn the system of the language and the color and tone of that language. The words he'll use and what they mean will be decided by those in his immediate world who will be teaching him. He's unable to read, of course, and therefore he'll learn his language orally. He is unaware that the language he learns will determine who he is, how he will see the world, how he will organize the world and how he will present his world to others.

All words have an intellectual content. We could have little difficulty defining, for instance, a "table" or a "home." But each word also has an emotional content. It becomes a very different thing when you are asked to define a "home" as opposed to telling about the "first home" you can remember. We all know the superficial meaning of the word "free." But if we were to try to define freedom in terms of ourselves in our present milieu, we would be hard-pressed.

Timothy Leary, when he was doing his interesting work in language and awareness, called words: "The imprint (the freezing) of external awareness." He explained that each time a parent or society teaches a child a new symbol he is given both an intellectual and an emotional content for the symbol. The content is limited by the attitudes and feelings of his parents and society. This process begins too early for the child to have much to say about what words will mean for him. Once "frozen," the attitudes and feelings toward the objects or person to which the words refer become very stable, in many cases irreversible. Through words, then, the child is given not only content but attitude. His attitudes of love are so formed. A sort of map is set up, Leary continues, which is static and upon which all subsequent learning of attitudes and awareness take place. The child's "map" will be determined by how closely the symbols resemble the facts and how they are taken in, assimilated, analyzed and reinforced through experience. The important language for establishing behavior, relationships, action, attitudes, empathy, responsibility, trust, caring, joy, response — the language of love, in other words, will thus be set.

From this point the child is still at the mercy of his teachers. He has been coerced, due to lack of experience and through his dependence, to trust his teachers and to accepting the love world they offer him as reality.

At about this time he goes to school. Great hope lies in education. Through education he's offered his first possible escape — broad, new worlds to discover, full of different, exceptional and exciting attitudes and definitions of life and love. But he's soon disillusioned. In place of freeing him to pursue his own world, he is now in a new environment often even less flexible than his home. Charles Reich makes this point dramatically in *The Greening of America:* "While the school's authority is lawless, school is nevertheless an experience made compulsory by the full power of the law, including criminal penalties. (The option to go to private school does exist for families that can afford it, but this is not the students' own option, and it is obviously available only to a few.) School has no prison bars, or locked doors like an insane asylum, but the student is no more free to leave it than a prisoner is free to leave the penitentiary."

With the child thus imprisoned, formal education assumes as its major task the process of passing on the "accumulated knowledge of the past," usually at the expense of the present and the future. It is a "feeding in" rather than a "leading out." Everything is taught but seemingly what is necessary for the growing individual's knowledge of self, of the relationship of his self to others. He finds many of his teachers lifeless individuals, devoid of enthusiasm, hope or joy. Erich Fromm said, "Living is the process of continuous rebirth. The tragedy in the life of most of us is that we die before we are fully born." Modern education does little to guide the child from death to rebirth.

Neither the love of self — what educators call self-respect — nor love of others — responsibility and love for his fellow man — can ever be taught in our present educational system. Teachers are too busy "managing" to be "creating." As Albert Einstein said, "It is nothing short of a miracle that instruction today has not strangled the holy curiosity of inquiry. For this delicate little plant lies mostly in need of freedom without which it will fall into rack and ruin and die without fail."

So the individual, now fully grown, leaves our schools confused, lonely, alienated, lost, angry, but with a mind full of isolated, meaningless facts which together are laughingly called an education. He knows neither who he is, where he is or how he got there. He has no concept of where he's going, how to arrive there nor what he'll do when he gets there. He has no idea what he has, what he wants, nor how to develop it. In essence, he's a type of robot — old before his time, living in the past, confused by the present, frightened by the future, much like the teachers who made him.

Nowhere along the way has he been directly exposed to love as a learned phenomenon. What he has learned of love he has come upon indirectly, by chance or by trial and error. His greatest exposure and often his only teaching has been through the commercial mass media which has always exploited love for its own ends. Frustrated poets with the aid of Metro-Goldwyn-Mayer and 20th Century Fox created Romantic Love for the world market. Their concept of love usually goes no deeper than boy meets girl, girl hassles boy (or vice-versa), boy loses girl, girl and boy gain insight through some magical stroke of fate, boy gets girl, and they live "happily ever after." All this with variation.

A classic case in point was the success of Rock Hudson-Doris Day films. Rock meets Doris. Rock woos Doris with attention; gifts, flowers, kind words, wild chases and special manners. Doris keeps running from Rock's advances for six reels. At last, Doris can resist no longer, she yields and gives herself to Rock. Rock carries Doris across the threshold. Fade out.

What would be most interesting would be to see what happens after the fade. Most certainly, any girl such as the character Doris portrays, who has run from a man for six reels, is frigid and any man who has put up with that kind of nonsense is impotent. They deserve each other.

Still, it's this example and countless others that create for us the notion of what love is.

Deodorant ads, cigarette commercials, cosmetic companies play an additional role in strengthening this insane notion of love. You are assured that love means running together through a meadow, lighting two cigarettes in the dark or applying a deodorant daily. You are given the idea that love just "happens," and usually at first sight. You don't have to work at love — love requires no teacher — you just fall into love — if you follow the right rules, and play the "game" correctly.

I would not want to form a partnership with an

architect who has only a little knowledge of building or a broker who has a limited knowledge of the stock market. Still, we form what we hope to be permanent relationships in love with people who have hardly any knowledge of what love is. They equate love with sex, attraction, need, security, romance, attention and a thousand similar things. Certainly, love is all of these and yet no one of these things. Someone in love class once said, "I wish she could love me more and need me less."

So most of us never learn to love at all. We play at love, imitate lovers, treat love as a game. Is it any wonder so many of us are dying of loneliness, feel anxious and unfulfilled, even in seemingly close relationships, and are always looking elsewhere for something more which we feel must certainly be there? "Is that all there is?" the song asks.

There is something else. It's simply this — the limitless potential of love within each person eager to be recognized, waiting to be developed, yearning to grow.

It's never too late to learn anything for which you have a potential. If you want to learn to love, then you must start the process of finding out what it is, what qualities make up a loving person and how these are developed. Each person has the potential for love. But potential is never realized without work. This does not mean pain. Love, especially, is learned best in wonder, in joy, in peace, in living.

MAN NEEDS
TO LOVE
AND BE LOVED

"*Scientists are discovering at this very moment that to live as if to live and love were one is the only way of life for human beings, because, indeed, this is the way of life which the innate nature of man demands.*"
—*Ashley Montagu.*

II.

It is true that in the last analysis each man stands alone. No matter how many people surround him or how famous he may be, in the most significant moments of his life he'll most likely find himself alone. The moment of birth is an "alone" world, as is the moment of death. In between these most significant moments there is the aloneness of the moments of tears, moments of struggle for change, moments of decision. These are times when man is faced only with himself, for no one else can ever truly understand his tears, his striving, or the complex motivations behind his decisions. Most men remain essentially strangers, even to those who love them. Orestes was alone when he decided to kill Clytemnestra, his mother, the act that freed him. Hamlet was alone when he made the decision to avenge his father's death, the act that destroyed him and virtually all those about him. John Kennedy was alone when he made the famous Bay of Pigs decision, a decision which might have brought another great war upon the world. Most of us will never know the weight of such momentous aloneness, but each time we, too, make a decision, insignificant though it may seem, we are just as truly alone.

The concept of aloneness becomes even more devastating when we equate "aloneness" with "loneliness." These, of course, are two radically different things. One can be alone and never feel loneliness and, conversely, one can be lonely even when he is among people. We have all experienced degrees of aloneness. They have not always been frightening. At times, we've found aloneness not only necessary but challenging, enlightening, even joyful. We've needed to be alone with ourselves to become reacquainted with ourselves in the deepest sense. We've needed time to reflect, to tie loose ends together, to make meaning of confusion or simply to revel in dreams. We have found that we often do these things best alone. Albert Schweitzer stressed this poignantly in his comment that modern man is so much a part of a crowd that he is dying of a personal loneliness.

Most men seem able to contend with the knowledge of being alone as a unique challenge. But they do not choose aloneness as a permanent state. Man is by nature a social being. He finds that he feels more comfortable in his aloneness to the degree to which he can volitionally be involved with others. He discovers that with each deep relationship he's brought closer to himself, that others help him to gain personal strength and this strength, in turn, makes it more possible for him to face his aloneness. So man strives consciously to reach out to others and bring them closer to himself. He does this to the degree to which he is able and to which he is accepted. The more he can ally himself to all things, even to death, the less fearful of isolation he becomes. For these reasons man created marriage, the family, communities, and most recently, communes, and some contend, even God.

There seems to be accumulating evidence that there is actually an inborn need for this togetherness, this human interaction, this love. It seems that without these close ties with other human beings, a newborn infant, for example, can regress, developmentally, lose consciousness, fall into idiocy and die. He may do this even if he has a perfect physical environment, a superb diet, and hospital-type hygiene. These do not seem to be enough for his continued physical and mental development. The infant mortality rate in well-equipped but understaffed institutions in the past decade has been appalling. In the previous two decades, before an understanding of the import of human response on child development was accepted, the statistics of infant mortality in institutions were even more horrible. In 1915, for example, at a meeting of the American Pediatric Society, Dr. Henry Chapin reported a study of ten institutions for infants in the United States where every child under two years of age died! Other reports at the time were similar.

Dr. Griffith Banning, in a study of 800 Canadian children, reported that in a situation where children whose parents were divorced, dead or separated, and where a feeling of love and affection was lacking, this knowledge did far more damage to growth than caused by disease and was more serious than all other factors combined.

Skeels, a noted psychologist and educator, reported recently on his most dramatic long-term study conducted on orphaned children where the only variable was human love and nurturing. One group of 12 children remained housed in an orphanage. Each of 12 children, in a second group, was brought daily to be cared for and loved by an adolescent, retarded girl in an institution nearby. His findings have become classic in the literature. After over twenty years of study he has found that of those in Group I who remained in the institution, without personal love, all were at present, if not dead, either in institutions for the mentally retarded or in institutions for the mentally ill. Of those in Group II, who received love and attention, all were self-supporting, most had graduated high school and all were happily married, with only one divorce. Startling statistics, indeed!

In New York City, Dr. Rene Spitz, in the past decade, studied children who lived in two different but physically adequate institutions. The institutions differed mainly in their approach to their charges in the amount of physical contact, and nurturing which the children received. In one institution the child was in contact with a human person, usually his mother, daily. In the second institution, there was a single nurse in charge of from eight to twelve children. Dr. Spitz studied each child in terms of factors of his development, medically and psychologically. He concerned himself with the child's Developmental Quotient which included such important aspects of personality as intelligence, perception, memory, imitative ability and so on. All else being comparatively equal in the children who had the nurturing, the caring human contact, the Developmental Quotient rose from 101.5 to 105 and showed a continued rising trend.

Those children deprived of nurturing started with an average Developmental Quotient of 124

Love is like a mirror. When you love another you become his mirror and he becomes yours. ...And reflecting each other's love you see infinity.

and by the second year of study the Developmental Quotient had fallen to a startling 45!

There are several other studies by Drs. Fritz Ridel, David Wineman, and Karl Menninger, all of which indicate a positive correlation between human concern and togetherness, and human growth and development. A very interesting and more thorough report on these studies and many of a similar nature can be found in a fascinating article by Ashley Montagu in the *Phi Delta Kappan*, May 1970.

So it seems the infant does not know or understand the subtle dynamics of love but already has such a strong need for it that the lack of it can affect his growth and development and even bring on his death. This need does not change with adulthood. In many cases, the need for togetherness and love becomes the major drive and goal of an individual's life. It is known that a lack of love is the major cause of severe neuroses and even psychoses in adulthood.

A few years back, I spent Sunday evenings on a rap-rock radio station in Los Angeles. It was an open line to the city. There were just two of us in a small, glass booth full of electrical equipment and outside, a sole telephone operator who managed six working lines. From 7:00 P.M. until 10:00 P.M. we talked to strange voices out of the city. The lines were never free, always one speaking, five waiting.

LOVE

The subject was love. It was interesting that the majority of calls concerned themselves with loneliness, inability to love others, confusion in interpersonal relationships, the fear of loving for fear of being hurt. Every one of the hundreds whose calls were received each evening wanted to love but found that they did not know how. One young man said, "I'm all alone in a small apartment on Melrose Avenue. There are all kinds of people like me on this street, everyone in his own apartment, all of us wanting to be with someone, none of us knowing how to break down the walls. What's the matter with us, anyway?"

In fact, the fear of aloneness and lack of love is so great in most of us that it's possible we can become a slave of this fear. If so we're ready to part with even our true self, anything, to meet others' needs and in this way hope to gain intimate companionship for ourselves.

There is a popular Broadway musical called *Company* which suggests that the only reason for love and marriage is so that one can have company, for better or for worse. It suggests that anything is better than nothing. In *Wild Palms*, William Faulkner has said, "If I were to choose between pain and nothing, I would choose pain." So do most men.

The child will comply with unreasonable rearing habits for the love of his parents. The adolescent will lose his identity, will part with his self, to be accepted as one of a group. He'll dress like his peers, wear his hair like them, listen to the same music, dance the same dances and take on the same attitudes. In adulthood, we find that the easiest way of being accepted is to be like those by whom we wish to be accepted. So we conform. We take up bridge, we read the same bestsellers, we give similar cocktail parties, construct like houses, dress properly according to group standards, so that we can feel the sense of community and security. During courtship and the period of romantic love, we'll change ourselves most radically for the approval and acceptance of the one we love, to the extent of the lyrics, "He likes curly hair and I never cared for curly, but he likes curly hair, so that's my weakness now."

In old age, we either will it or are forced to move into artificial environments for the aged to escape from a youthful world where we seem to be no longer useful or wanted, into a world where we can continue to feel one with the group.

No matter how much we deny it, we find that at every stage of life we move toward others — to parents when we are a child, to peers when we are adolescents, to possible sexual partners when young adults, to appropriate communities when adults, and to retirement communities when we are older — on to our death.

LOVE

We need others. We need others to love and we need to be loved by them. There is no doubt that without it, we too, like the infant left alone, would cease to grow, cease to develop, choose madness and even death.

A QUESTION OF DEFINITION

"Love is patient and kind; love is not jealous, or conceited, or proud; love is not ill-mannered, or selfish, or irritable; love does not keep a record of wrongs: love is not happy with evil, but is happy with the truth. Love never gives up: its faith, hope and patience never fail. Love is eternal...There are faith, hope and love, these three; but the greatest of these is love."

—*I Corinthians 13.*

To a great extent, the job of dealing with love is left to poets, philosophers and holy men. Scientists seem to avoid the subject. Abraham Maslow has stated: "It is amazing how little the empirical sciences have to offer on the subject of love. Particularly strange is the silence of the psychologists. Sometimes it is merely sad or irritating, as in the case of the text-books of psychology and sociology, particularly none of which recognizes the subject."

Pitirim Sorokin, the famed Harvard sociologist, in his book, *The Ways and Power of Love,* explains why he feels the scientist has long avoided the discussion of love. He states: "The sensate minds emphatically disbelieve in the power of love. It appears to us something illusionary. We call it self-deception, the opiate of people's minds, idealistic bosh, unscientific delusion. We are biased against all theories that try to prove the power of love and other positive forces in determining human behavior and personality; in influencing the course of biological, social, mental and moral evolution; in affecting the direction of historical events; in shaping social institutions and culture. In the sensate milieu they appear to be unconvincing, unscientific, prejudiced and superstitious."

So, science and scientists remain silent on the subject. Some recognize it as a reality while others see it only as a fantasized construct to give a meaningless life *meaning*. Some condemn it as out-and-out pathological.

There is no doubt that love is not an easy subject with which to deal. Perhaps to be concerned with it is to "walk in where angels fear to tread." But for such a powerful life force to remain ignored, uninvestigated, condemned by the social scientists, is ludicrous.

Perhaps the fears are founded in a semantic base. There is perhaps no word more misused than love. Francois Villon, the French Romantic poet, decried the fact that we constantly "beggar the poor love word to base kitchen usages and work-a-day desires." A person may "love" God and "love" apple pie or the Dodgers. He may see "love" as sacrifice or dependency. He may think of "love" only in a male-female relationship; as a referent to sexual "love"; or he may see it only in saintly purity.

We are obliged as individuals to arrive at some understanding of love before we can deal with it. This, as we indicated earlier, is not an easy task and we're often satisfied with giving it but small consideration. The task may even seem to us impossible and limiting of so broad a concept. For the scientist, therefore, it seems better to ignore it altogether.

It has, then, fallen into the hands of the saint who defines it in terms of a state of ectasy; the poet who sees it in an exaggerated state of joy or disillusionment; the philosopher who attempts to analyze it in his rational, point-by-point, often obscure fashion. Love, it seems, fits perfectly into no one of these molds, for it may be all at once; a state of ecstasy, a state of joy, a state of disillusionment, a rational state or an irrational state.

Love is many things, perhaps too many things to be definitive about it. So, one who attempts a definition runs the danger of ending up being vague or nebulous and arriving nowhere.

We have already said that each man has learned and continues to learn love in a most individual and unique fashion. To expect him to understand the word when used by another, in anything but a general sense, is to expect the miraculous. If one says to another, "I love apple pie," there would be little doubt what the person meant. Namely, that apple pie appealed to his gastronomic tastes. But, if the same person were to say to the other, "I love you," this would be another matter. We would have a tendency to question: "What does he mean by that? Does he love my body? My mind? Does he love me at this moment? Forever?" And so on. A student in love class stated this precisely when she said, "The difference between saying, 'I love you' to a friend or a lover is that if you said 'I love you' to a friend, the friend would know exactly what you meant."

It's certainly clear to the reader who has come this far, that to define love presents monumental problems because one grows in love, so his definition changes, and enlarges. But there are certain things which can be said about love, certain common elements which can be examined and which may help in clarifying the subject for discussion. Sharing some ideas regarding these aspects of love is my purpose in writing this book.

Love is a learned, emotional reaction. It is a response to a learned group of stimuli and behaviors. Like all learned behavior, it is effected by the interaction of the learner with his environment, the person's learning ability, and the type and strength of the reinforcers present; that is, which people respond, how they respond and to what degree they respond to his expressed love.

Love is a dynamic interaction, lived every second of our lives, all of our lives. Therefore, it is everywhere at every time. For this reason, I am put off by the phrase, "to fall *in* love." I do not believe that one falls *in* or *out* of love. One learns to react in a particular way to a certain degree to a specific stimulus. That reaction will be the visible index of his love. He possesses no more love to "fall into" or "out of" than what he has and acts out at any precise moment of his life. It seems more accurate to say one *grows* in love. The more he learns, the more his opportunities to change his behavorial responses and thus expand his ability to love. Man is either constantly *growing* in love, or dying. Therefore, his actions as well as his interactions will change throughout his life.

If one wishes to know love, one must live love, in action. To think or read about love or carry on profound discourses on love is all very well, but in the last analysis, will offer few if any real answers. Thoughts, readings and discourses on love are of value only as they present questions to be *acted upon*. One will learn love only with fresh insight, with each new bit of knowledge, which he *acts out*, and which is reacted to, or his knowledge is valueless. As Rilke states so accurately, he must simply

One does not fall 'in' or 'out' of love.
One grows in love.

"love along someday into the answer." One, in other words, lives the questions. But in order to live the questions, it is logical that one will have to pose them.

In living the questions he will learn many truths about love, among them that love is not a thing. It's not a commodity that can be bartered for or bought or sold, nor can it be forced upon or from someone. It can only voluntarily be given away. If an individual chooses to share it with all men alike, he's free to do so. If he chooses to reserve it for a unique few, he may do this, also. His love is his to give.

There are people available for purchase, body and mind, in the name of love. But it's only a self-deceiver who believes that love can truly be bought. He may buy another's body, his time, his earthly possessions, but he will never buy his love. One may choose to pretend love for a price. This is a dramatic art which has been perfected by many to the extent to which it is impossible for anyone to discern the deceit. But this game of playing love is not easy. The cost is great and never worth the price.

Love cannot be captured or tied to a wall. Love only slips through the chains. If love wills to take another course, it goes; and all the prisons, guards, chains or obstructions in the world aren't strong enough to detain it for a second. If one human being ceases to will to grow in love with another, the

*Love is always open arms. If you
close your arms about love you will
find that you are left holding
only yourself.*

other may play several parts to hold him. He may become a villain and threaten him; he may become generous and offer him gifts; he may become the schemer and make him feel guilty; he may become crafty and trick him into remaining, or he may change his own "self" to meet the other's needs. But whatever he does the other's love is gone and he will receive, for all of his energies, only an empty body, devoid of love — all but dead. So the prize for his efforts will be to live out his life holding on desperately and giving his love to a lifeless, loveless human frame. This, though it may seem revolting, is common practice, often performed for security, fame or fortune. The dynamics become even more grotesque when one considers that this dead-ended relationship forfeits all possibilities of a lover's continued growth. Love is always open arms. With arms open you allow love to come and go as it wills, freely, for it'll do so anyway. If you close your arms about love you'll find you are left only holding yourself.

Love, of some type and degree, is present in all civilized men. A base for love and the potential for growth in love is also present in each man. Love is then a process of "building upon" what is already there. Love is never complete in any person. There is always room for growth. At each point in a person's life, his love is at a different level of development as well as in the process of becoming. It is foolish to feel that one's love is ever completely realized or actualized. Perfect love is rare indeed. It is to be wondered if any man has ever achieved it. This does not mean that it may not be possible, nor a goal devoutly to be strived for. In fact, it is our greatest challenge, *for love and the self are one and the discovery of either is the realization of both*.

He will perceive also that there are not "kinds" of love. Love is only of one kind. Love is love. One knows and expresses and acts out what he knows of love. He does this at each stage of growth. It's like the child. When he's born he knows little of love and all objects are loved equally. As he grows in love, he differentiates with the growing knowledge he has and chooses responsive objects upon which to test his love. He loves his Pablum; he also loves his mother. His mother is more responsive and satisfying than his Pablum, it is hoped. So he grows more deeply in love with his mother. There are degrees of love, but there's only one kind of love.

He will discover that love is trusting. Experience seems to convince us that only fools trust, that only fools believe and accept all things. If this is true, then love is most foolish, for if it is not founded on trust, belief and acceptance, it's not love. Erich Fromm has said, "Love means to commit oneself without guarantee, to give oneself completely in the hope that our love will produce love in the loved person. Love is an act of faith, and whoever is of little faith is also of little love." The perfect love would be one that gives all and expects nothing. It would, of course, be willing and delighted to take anything it was offered; the more the better. But it would ask for nothing. For if one expects nothing and asks nothing, he can never be deceived or disappointed. It is only when love demands that it brings on pain.

This statement sounds very basic and simple, but in practice, it's difficult, indeed. There are few of us so strong, so totally permissive, so trusting, as to give without expectation. It is not surprising, since we are taught from infanthood to anticipate a reward for any effort expended. If we work, we demand a proper wage or we will quit. If we cultivate plants and trees, we expect flowers and fruits or we will chop them down. If we invest time in a task, we await some satisfaction or praise or we refuse to do it again. In fact, a demonstrated reward is often the sole motivation for learning.

But love isn't like that. It's only love when given without expectation. For instance, you can't insist that someone you love, love you back. Even the thought is comical. Yet, unconsciously, it's the manner in which most people live. If you love truly, then you have no choice but to believe, trust, accept and hope that your love will be returned. But there can never be any assurance, never any guarantee. If one waits to love only until he is certain of receiving equal love in return, he may wait forever. Indeed, if he loves with any expectation at all, he will surely be disappointed eventually, for it's not likely that most people can meet all of his needs even if their love for him is great.

One loves because he wills it, because it gives him joy, *because he knows that growth and discovery of oneself depend upon it*. He knows that the only assurance he has lies within himself. If he trusts and believes in himself, he will trust and believe others. He's eager to accept all they are able to give, but he can be certain of and depend upon nothing except himself.

The Buddhist says that you are well on your way to enlightenment when you "cease desiring." Perhaps we can never reach this enviable state of peace, but to the extent to which we can live without demanding or expecting (except from ourselves), so can we be free from disillusionment and disappointment. To expect something from another because it's our right, is to court unhappiness. Others can and will only give what they are able, not what you desire they give. When you cease placing conditions on your love you have taken a giant step toward learning to love.

The human seeking love will find that love is patient. The lover knows that each person can enhance his knowledge of love and bring him closer to himself. He knows that experience and the knowledge people have of love differs. He's excited by the idea that a relationship is a sharing, a mutual revealing of one's knowledge of love. He knows that each man has an endless capacity to love, but that capacity will be realized differently in every man. Each person will grow at his own rate, in his own manner, at his own time, by way of his unique self. Therefore, it's helpless to berate, judge, predict, demand or assume. Love must be patient. Love waits. This doesn't mean that love sits passively forever, if necessary, for the person to grow. Love is active, not passive. It is continually engaged in the process of opening new doors and windows so that fresh ideas and questions can be admitted. It shares in knowledge and offers a proving ground for trying out what's learned. It sets an appetizing, attractive, gourmet table, but it cannot force anyone to eat. It allows each the freedom to select and reject according to his taste. Love offers itself as a continual feast to be nourished upon, knowing that the more one samples, the more one ingests and digests, the greater become his energies. One can't overeat. He will only have more to offer when others come to his feast. Love's potential is limitless.

Love has a different manner of revealing itself through each man. To expect others to love as you do at the moment is unrealistic. Only you are you and can therefore respond to love, give love and feel love as you do. The adventure lies in the discovery

Love offers itself as a continual feast to be nourished upon.

of love in yourself and others. In watching love in others revealing itself, the soft, wondrous disclosure; the gentle, guarded unfolding.

Love isn't afraid to feel and cries for expression. Cultures vary in their attitudes about emotional demonstrativeness. In some cultures the cries of the family at a funeral are expected. Friends would be surprised and shocked if it were otherwise. In other cultures, a calm, austere approach to death is highly approved and the show of emotion would be surely frowned upon. In America, for instance, most children are taught to "control" their emotions, to internalize their feelings. To be demonstrative, to laugh uproariously or weep bitterly are signs of immaturity. Only babies cry.

It isn't surprising then that the adult finds it difficult to express strong feelings such as love. It's difficult for him to verbalize what he feels; he doesn't have the words or the practice. Latin lovers, for instance, have the reputation of being able to wax poetic appropriately to each new love. This is often revealed in the richness of emotionally-laden words to be found in their languages. French, Italian, Spanish are examples of such "romance" languages. To his words he often adds animation and gesticulation which enhance their emotional content. One can often understand such a person merely by observation, without a single word being understood.

LOVE

Strong emotions are present in all people. Without feeling, we would not be human. It's unnatural for man to hide what he's feeling, though if taught to do so, he can learn. Love teaches a man to show what he is feeling. Love never presupposes that it can be discerned or felt without expression.

Each time I return to my relatives in Italy, there's no doubt about their love so sweetly and warmly expressed. I instantaneously feel their excitement, and joy at my presence. I am caught up in their cries of happiness, exclamations of love, hugs, kisses, fondling, all affirmations of their feelings. I find this refreshing and delightful. I was raised in such an environment. My family always showed what they felt, openly expressed it. But it's understandable that for those who are unaccustomed to such a shower of feelings, this experience can be an overwhelmingly frightening and even a depressing one.

Tears are all but disappearing in our culture. Certainly, a man doesn't cry and even a woman is considered "emotional" if she weeps. So we must all cry alone or risk the title of "neurotic" or "odd."

Recently, while viewing *Man From La Mancha*, the musical based upon *Don Quixote*, the novel of Cervantes, I found myself caught up in the trials of the poor misunderstood, ill-treated knight. It wasn't difficult to relate to his need for recelebration of the beautiful, the romantic and the good in a world where these were no longer considered of value. During his death scene, surrounded by those he loved, Quixote rose up, grabbed his lance, and was again ready to charge windmills for the love of his Dulcinea. The scene affected me greatly and tears flowed freely down my cheeks. A woman seated next to me poked her husband and whispered in wonder, "Look, Honey, that man's crying!" Hearing this, I took out my handkerchief and loudly blew my nose as I continued to sob. She was so full of disbelief that a grown man could cry that I feel certain, to this day, she has no idea how the show ended. Love isn't afraid to feel.

As human persons, we're even more separated, physically. All over Europe and Asia, women and men alike kiss, embrace and walk hand-in-hand, arm-in-arm. There are certain cities in the United States where these acts would be considered a misdemeanor and such men and women would be jailed. Touching is still permitted among women, but strictly prohibited, from childhood, among males. Yet this touching offers a form of communication often far greater than words and expression. To put your arm about another or on his shoulder is a way of saying, "I see you," "I feel with you," "I care." I have seen persons cry while others look on in uneasy embarrassment. Someone may offer a handkerchief, but seldom an embrace.

Babies and dogs are common visitors to love class. One young lady made the observation, "It's funny, but no one hesitates touching a baby and patting or hugging a strange dog. And here I sit sometimes dying to have someone touch me and no one does." At this, she passed among the students on all fours and, needless to say, her request was fulfilled. She concluded that perhaps it was necessary, though it seemed a shame, for the human being to let his needs be known. "I guess," she said, "that we don't trust letting people know the fact that we all like to be touched because we're afraid that people will misinterpret. So we sit back in loneliness and physical isolation." Love has a need to be expressed physically.

Love lives the moment. Most people are either living in yesterday or busily working for tomorrow. They look back to "the good old days" with fondness and try to find in the present the security of the past. They soon discover that they are standing still and don't realize that in our fast-moving world, to stand still is to move backward, and to move backward, is to die. The past is dead, it is unreal. It has value only as it affects the moment.

Other people live for tomorrow. They amass fortunes and store them away. They deny themselves daily to buy large insurance policies. They direct their entire process of life to some nebulous future or to death itself. They are so concerned with tomorrow that they have lost the purpose of life. They forget that there are no permanent goals.

A Question Of Definition

When they have a goal and reach it, they only find another to take its place. The Tomorrow they plan for never comes. Tomorrow only comes with death. Life is not the goal, it is the process. It is the "getting there, not the arrival." Thoreau said, "Oh God, to have reached the point of death only to find that you have never lived at all." So it is for him who lives only in unreality that the past is dead or the future never comes.

There is only the moment. The now. Only what you are experiencing at this second is real. This does not mean, live for the moment. It means you live *the* moment. A very different thing. There's value in the past. After all, it brought you to where you are. There's value in the future, but it lies in the dream, for who can predict tomorrow? Only the moment has true value, for it's here. Love knows this — it doesn't look back — it experiences the past and takes the best from it. It doesn't look forward. It knows that tomorrow's dream remains waiting and may never come. Love is now! It is only in the "now" that love is reality. Love has meaning only as it is experienced in the now. If one is looking at a flower, he is one with the flower; if one is reading, he is totally absorbed; if one is listening to music, he goes with the sound; if one is talking or listening to another, he is the other.

There's an old Buddhist *koan* which relates the story of a monk who's running from a hungry bear.

Love has meaning only as it is
experienced in the "now."

A Question Of Definition

He runs to a cliff and is required to jump or be eaten. As he falls, he grabs hold of a small clump of wood extending from the wall of the cliff. He looks down to find a starving tiger awaiting his fall. At that moment from the side of the cliff, come two hungry gophers who start at once to gnaw at the clump of wood from which he is suspended. There he is, hungry bear above, starving tiger below, and gophers to the side. Looking beyond the gophers, he sees a bush of wild strawberries and a giant, red, ripe, juicy one facing him, ready to be eaten. He plucks it and puts it in his mouth and eats it, exclaiming, "How delicious!" Love revels in and grows in the moment and the joy of the moment.

So we find love is many things, though we know it's not a thing in the sense that it cannot be bought or sold or weighed or measured. Love can only be given, expressed freely. It can't be captured or held, for it's neither there to tie nor to hold. It's in everyone and everything in varying degrees and awaits actualization. It's not apart from the self. Love and the self are one. There are not kinds of love, love is love; there are only degrees of love. Love is trusting, accepting and believing, without guarantee. Love is patient and waits, but it's an active waiting, not a passive one. For it is continually offering itself in a mutual revealing, a mutual sharing. Love

LOVE

is spontaneous and craves expression through joy, through beauty, through truth, even through tears. Love lives the moment; it's neither lost in yesterday nor does it crave for tomorrow. Love is Now!

LOVE KNOWS NO AGE

"*Who has drunk will drink, who has dreamed will dream. He will not give up that alluring abyss, that sound of the fathomless, that entrance into the forbidden, that effort to handle the impalpable and to see the invisible; he returns to it, bends over it, he takes one step forward, then two; and thus it is that one penetrates into the impenetrable and there it is that one finds the boundless release of infinite meditation.*"

—*Victor Hugo.*

"*There is no love where there is no will.*"

—*Gandhi.*

IV.

Man can learn, relearn or unlearn to the point of death. There is always more to discover. No matter how much knowledge he has, man can never know everything about anything. For this reason, the semanticist says all sentences should end with, "and, etc."

Change is the end result of all true learning. Change involves three things: First, a dissatisfaction with self — a felt void or need; second, a decision to change — to fill the void or need, and; third, a conscious dedication to the process of growth and change — the willful act of making the change, doing something.

Man is forever expressing his loneliness, his despair, his frustration, his loss of hope. In his day-to-day living he finds it difficult to share, to understand and to relate with others. He feels that he must cope with an inordinate amount of envy, fear, anxiety and hate. He's constantly finding reasons for his unhappiness in those about him and in his external environment: "The political system is corrupt and will always be so." "Wars are inevitable." "Man is essentially evil and cannot change." "Justice, peace and security is only for the wealthy; the common man is just a dupe of the system." "Education is meaningless for the future, frozen into its own irrelevance." "Existence is a dead-end street where death stands holding a bloody knife. There are no detours, no escapes."

He sees himself as helpless in a situation that is hopeless. He appears intent upon looking for gloom. He seems more willing to accept the negative than the positive, always more prepared to doubt than trust. He is continually living in worry about the future and disillusionment regarding the past. He seldom finds himself at the source of his unhappiness. He scoffs at the idea that he can also elect happiness. In fact, man may be the only living creature with sufficient will and intelligence to choose happiness. How sad that he so often chooses despair. An optimist is seen as a fool. A lover is seen as a helpless romantic. If one enjoys life he's called a "ne'er-do-well." Man gets the feeling that if he's joyful, he is certain to be punished for it tomorrow. The old adage that says, "All that's good in the world is either illegal, immoral or fattening," is a case in point. The Christian ethic that convinces man that he is not on earth to know joy and satisfaction but rather to work and suffer his way to eternal peace with God, is another illustration. Man seldom questions the fact that ugliness and evil are to be found in the world. But he's never as ready to accept that life also offers unlimited beauty and potential for joy as well as endless opportunities for pleasure.

Man becomes dissatisfied with himself and placing the blame on the unalterable aspects of a hostile world, he feels comfort in his self-created hopelessness. In this way, he relieves himself of all responsibility.

I am not suggesting that there is no evil in the world, nothing to fear, no corruption, no hatred, no malice, no animosity. One need only pick up any newspaper, watch any television screen, read any modern novel, or follow the world political scene to find all the unpleasantness and injustice he needs to reinforce a negative attitude.

But most men fail to consider that there are at least *two* major forces at work upon him in the complicated process of his adjustment. Certainly he must contend with the external forces, the natural forces. An earthquake, flood or bolt of lightning may destroy him or those he loves. An accident may permanently cripple him. But how he responds, reacts and lives with the handicap or through the earthquake or flood is another matter. This he can regulate. This he has some management over. Man has will and thus to a large measure guides his life. The devastating effects of external forces are not often experienced in a lifetime. So he is free to use his internal powers to make his own life. He can write his own dialogue, surround himself with the actors of his choice, paint his backdrop and arrange his background music. Then, if he doesn't like the play he has created for himself, he has only himself to blame. But even then he has choice. He can get off the stage and produce a new play. A free man is free even in the darkest prison. Most people in despair have little knowledge and less will with which to make things better for themselves. They are convinced that things are unalterable and will remain that way forever. As long as man has will he will have some degree of control over his reactions, responses and conclusions. To this extent he can assume responsibility for his own life. He is not totally at the mercy of forces greater than himself for he himself becomes a powerful force.

In order to change, then, man must trust that he is capable of change. If he is dissatisfied with his ability to live in love, for example, then he must face this fact but be convinced that he is able to do something about it.

Knowing that one is always capable of change, the second step lies in making the decision to change. Change does not occur by merely willing it any more than behavior changes simply through insight. One can know that something is evil, painful or dangerous and still pursue it relentlessly. One can only move toward change when he willfully arrives at a proposal to do so. The obese gentleman who wants desperately to be slim and handsome in his bathing suit cannot do it by desire alone. He must plan a proper diet, stay on his diet, and engage in the right exercise. Otherwise, his wish will never become reality. He has the insight about how to achieve his goal, but until the moment of action all of his insight goes for naught. "To be is to do," says the existentialist. "One only becomes real (human) at the point of action." If one wants to love, it is apparent that he must move to love.

The third step in change is perhaps the most difficult. It involves the actual processes of the relearning. All learning involves searching, finding, analyzing, evaluating, experiencing, accepting, rejecting, practice and reinforcement. It is often said that "love is its own reward." If this means that by being a loving human being, one gets all the reinforcement he needs, it is only partially true. It

A total immersion in life offers the best classroom for learning to love.

means, also, that since society and man are often less than perfect, one is going to have, at times, to reinforce himself in order to continue to learn. The lover must often say, "I love because I must, because I will it. I love for myself, not for others. I love for the joy it gives me — and incidentally, only — for that joy it gives to others. If they reinforce me it will be good. If they do not, it will be good, for I *will* to love."

As in learning all things, man must be constantly alert, watchful, patient, observant, trusting, open-minded and not easily discouraged. He must be willing to experiment and be constantly evaluating and flexible. Life, and experiencing through the total immersions in living, offers the best classroom for learning to love. Even the greatest guru cannot give you love. He can only help by guiding you, by offering insights, suggestions and encouragement. You will not learn either by watching others live love; you will only learn as an active participant in love.

If one is dissatisfied, then, with his ability to live in love, it is good, for it may be the first step in finding the love he craves. But this is only a beginning. He must also will to change and move to change. Learning is a complicated life-long process. To learn to love is to be in constant change. The process is endless, for man's potential to love is infinite.

LOVE HAS MANY DETERRENTS

"Just because the message may never be received does not mean it is not worth sending."
—Segaki
Trans. David Stackton.

V.

Loving is never easy and the man who has decided to live in love is liable to find many barriers to his growing in love. But if he analyzes them carefully and astutely, he will be likely to discover that they are all artificial obstacles and mostly of his own making. In reality, they do not exist. They are, for the most part, simply excuses for not accepting the challenge of love. The man who falls a dupe to these deterrents condemns himself forever to remain much less than a total human being.

There is ample reason for man to blame his

inability to love on factors apart from himself. He can insist, for example, that others are basically corrupt, depraved and unable to change. Therefore, would he not be foolish to try to influence them in any way? He can accuse man of being hostile by nature. Then isn't his decision to avoid contact with others well formulated, unless he is a fool, seeking to be hurt? He can point up that the endless obstructions which lie in the way of love are insurmountable and historically have always been. Would not his trying to remove these barriers be like an insect trying to change the course of a giant river? A waste of time and energy! Or he may sit back comfortably in the assurance that he is already a lover, satisfied with his ability to love and be loved. Would he not be foolish, then, to gamble his present security for a doubtful future?

Man often hides comfortably behind these easily reinforced rationalizations for his entire life. He never sees their relationship to his inability to form serious, meaningful relationships or feel peak experiences.

If he creates an image of man as basically hostile and evil, for example, he is wise to be hesitant to reveal himself, much less reveal his love for him, for in doing so, he becomes susceptible to hurt. It's easier and safer for him to sit alone, even if he feels a natural urge to relate to others, than run the risk of being shunned. His first assumption, of course, is that others will reject him. He seldom considers the fact that he runs an equal chance of being accepted. It does not seem possible to him that the person at the next table or across the room may have as great a need for him as he has for them. He elects to remain silent, alone and lonely and states as his basic defense, "What if I approach him and he turns away?" He seldom asks, "What if I extend my hand to another and he reciprocates with, 'Yes, please join me.'"

I recall an evening in a bar in San Francisco. I was with several good friends. The conversation was animated. We were all sharing reactions to a wondrous day's diversions. I saw a gentleman at a nearby table, sitting alone, staring at his half-filled cocktail glass. "Why don't we ask him to join us? He seems so alone," I said. "I know what it means to be alone in a room full of people."

"Leave him be," was the consensus of the others. "Perhaps he wants to be alone."

"That's fine, but if I ask him, he'll have a choice."

I approached the gentleman and questioned whether he would like to join us or if he would prefer being alone. His eyes lit up with surprise. He accepted happily. He was a visitor from Germany. As he joined our table, he told us that he had traveled the entire length of the United States without speaking to anyone except hotel receptionists, tour guides and waiters. Our invitation was a most welcome change.

Of course, it must be admitted that some of the fault rested with the German gentleman, for part of the responsibility lies with each of us to reach out. If we take the risk, it is true that we may be rejected, but we must also remember that all men are also prospective friends and lovers.

We tend to suspect man of evil more readily than of good. The evil about him makes the news media, the good seldom does. Considering the world's population, there are relatively few murders, robberies, rapes or major crimes. But when a crime does occur, we are certain to hear of it. Not simply because it's news, but rather because it sells newspapers. People seem to enjoy the sensational and find some pleasure in revulsion. But, in reality, the greater number of men are like ourselves. They do not voluntarily hurt another human being, steal from him or kill him. They can usually be trusted, are concerned and are friendly. Most live their lives without having to deal with police, courts of law or lawyers. This fact is taken, rather, as what is to be expected of man. The evil he does, on the other hand, is magnified. It is of interest for it is the deviation. But we act, often, as if the deviation is the rule. Perhaps the greatest tribute to the good in man was paid by the young Anne Frank, a Jewess who literally spent most of her short life hiding from the Nazis in a small apartment in Amsterdam and finally met her death at their hands. She was still able to write in her diary shortly before her murder: "No matter. I still believe that at heart man is good."

Man learns evil in the same manner in which he learns good. If he believes in a world of evil he will respond suspiciously, fearfully and be constantly searching for and assuredly finding the evil he seeks. If, on the other hand, he believes in a world of good, he will remain confident, trusting, vulnerable and hopeful. To discern only the evil in the world and live willingly in its shadow, is to set up another obstacle to love.

Another deterrent to love is the rationalization that there are too many forces prohibiting a sane person from loving. Though man, by nature, is a creator, he creates life and builds upon knowledge. He is often taught from an early age that his very survival depends upon his ability to destroy. He is pictured as being constantly at the mercy of a series of possible destructive forces. In fact, it is made to seem as if destroyers are those who actually thrive in the culture. It is understandable, then, that he has little incentive to use his creative strength to battle the forces of destruction. It seems so hopeless. Man is happiest when he is creating. In fact, the highest state of which man is capable lies in the creative

Real love always creates, it never destroys. In this, lies man's only promise.

act. Love always creates, it never destroys. In this lies man's only promise.

Thornton Wilder ends his amazing little philosophical novel, *The Bridge of San Luis Rey*, with the following statement: "There is a land of the living and a land of the dead. The bridge is love; the only truth, the only survival."

If man looks at the unloving and unloved in the world, the problem seems so overwhelming it often causes him to completely give up hope. If he studies the past, he finds that selfishness, greed, wretchedness and affliction have existed since the beginning of history. He is convinced that men have always, assumes therefore, will always, covet more and different things and fight among themselves to acquire them; Catholic against Protestant against Jew, Communists against Socialists against Capitalists, rich against poor against middle class, black against white against yellow, genius against intelligent against ignorant. His proof and support rests in the argument that it has always been, so it always will be and he as an individual is helpless to change it. It's true that the problems of poverty, starvation, wars, ignorance, prejudice, fears, and antipathy are with us in abundance. There are few individuals who have the power to stop prejudice, universal poverty or world wars, but this is not the question. The only question we can justly ask of ourselves is, "What can *I* do?" The answer is usually simple and answerable, especially if we truly care and are willing to assume the responsibility.

I met a young Chinese refugee in Hong Kong. He was one of a family of eleven, all of whom were on the point of starvation. Though he had some knowledge of English, he wanted desperately to learn so as to be able to secure a well-paying position in the city. By my contributing a few dollars for books and enrolling him in the English Speaking Society, he was able to find the means of bringing his family back to a well-functioning unit. He was determined to repay me upon graduation. I refused and asked him to find another youth, like himself, and offer him a similar chance. To date, we have sent three young men through school. I have not in this way solved the refugee problem in Hong Kong, but I have helped three families to survive. If each person were to assume a small responsibility, things could be made better. Helping through large charity systems is fine, but it has lost its personal value, its joy and satisfaction in perceiving and experiencing the results. Things can be changed. Nothing is irreversible. Perhaps I personally cannot do much about the infant mortality rate or the problems of the aged, but I may give some of my time to making a child's day or an elderly person's remaining days on earth more pleasant.

A little knowledge of love and the satisfaction therewith is also a deterrent to growth in love. If man finds that he has the love of a few in his life and if he is able to love them in return, he assumes that is all he needs to know of love or can expect to find. What else can there be? He does not suspect that love is illimitable, deep, infinite and that the potential for greater security, joy and growth is his. He does not think about the possibility that at another place, at that moment, there is someone in need of his love. It often takes a severe emotional shock to awaken man from his lethargic state. Let's say he now has a wife whom he loves and who loves him; they have a fair sex life; two children who are growing in his image; a home with thick walls and large locks to protect him from the outside world; a good job, and some money in the bank to secure his future. He has everything. But what happens, as in the story of Job, if one thing after the other falls about him? His children drop out and join a hippy commune; his wife finds a lover; he loses his position, his walls tumble; the bank crumbles; or his locks are picked? He has several choices. He may endeavor to find the same life again, which is impossible. One can never relive anything, for it remains always, at best, only a poor copy of the original. He may go mad or take his life. He may become bitter and live without trust, hope or concern. Or, he has the choice to learn from his encounter, grow from the experience and start afresh, with new knowledge, hope, possibilities and alternatives.

When change confronts man he often uses the excuse that he's too old to change, too old to learn. He says, "You can't teach an old dog new tricks." This analogy when directed to man is as condescending as it is untrue. Even an "old dog" can learn new tricks. The real issue is that he lacks motivation or is simply too lazy. Man's ability to learn will always be greater than that of the "old dog" and to compare them, is to degrade the very strength that keeps a dog a dog but makes man human.

Each day we are offered new means for learning and growing in love. Each day in which we become more observant, more flexible, more knowledgeable, more aware, we grow in love. Even the seemingly most insignificant thing can bring us closer to ourselves and therefore to others. If, at each moment, we listen and learn — the seagulls' cry on a deserted, windy beach will tell us as much about life, living and death, as the tragedy which destroys our home and loved ones. As the Japanese *haiku* says, "My barn having burned to the ground, I can now see the moon." There is insight, knowledge and discovery in the barn as well as the moon. Now the farmer knows both.

One must never be satisfied with his ability to love. No matter where he is, it is always just a beginning.

Finally, a great deterrent to love is found in anyone who fears change, for as suggested above, growing, learning, experiencing is change. Change is inevitable. There is only one thing of which you can be certain and that is change. To deny change is to deny the only single reality. Attitudes change, feelings change, desires change, especially love changes. There is no stopping it, no holding it back; there is only going with it. There is a Hindu tale about a man in a small boat rowing up a fast-flowing river against the current. After a great battle, he finally discovers that the effort is futile, so he gives up, raises his oars and begins to sing. The moment teaches him a new way of life; only when he goes with the changing river is man truly free.

Deterrents to love are man-made. Love will not be deterred. Love flows like the river; always itself, yet ever changing, recognizing no obstacle.

TO
LOVE OTHERS
YOU MUST FIRST
LOVE
YOURSELF

"We are one, after all, you and I, together we suffer, together exist, And forever will recreate each other."

—*Teilhard de Chardin.*

VI.

To love others you must love yourself. We have already stated several times that you can only give to others what you have yourself. This is especially true of love. You cannot give what you have not learned and experienced. Since love is not a thing, it is not lost when given. You can offer your love completely to hundreds of people and still retain the same love you had originally. It is like knowledge. The wise man can teach all he knows and when he's through he'll still know all that he has taught. But first he must have the knowledge. It would better be said that man "shares" love, as he "shares" knowledge but he can only share what he possesses.

Loving oneself does not imply an ego-centered reality like the old witch in *Snow White* who reveled in the process of gazing into her mirror and asking, "Mirror, mirror on the wall, who is the fairest one of all." Loving oneself does mean a genuine interest, caring, concern and respect for oneself. To care about oneself is basic to love. Man loves himself when he sees himself with accuracy, genuinely appreciates what he sees, but is especially excited and challenged with the prospect of what he can become.

Each man is unique. Nature abhors sameness. Each flower in the field is different, each blade of grass. Have you ever seen two roses alike, even among the same variety? No two faces are exactly alike, even in identical twins. Our fingerprints are so singularly ours that we can be positively identified by them. But man is a strange creature. Diversity frightens him. Instead of accepting the challenge, the joy, the wonder of variation, he usually is frightened of it. He either moves away from or endeavors to twist uniqueness into sameness. Only then does he feel secure.

Each child born is an unmarked creation, a new combination of wonder. In general, his human anatomy is similar to others, but on a subtle level even how his anatomy functions will vary with each individual. His personality development seems to have common elements which affect it; heredity, environment, chance. But there is surely an additional element, not yet scientifically identifiable, which can be called the "X" factor of personality, that special combination of forces which act upon the individual so that he will react, respond, perceive as himself, alone. The child is exceptional but most learning which he will receive from birth will not afford him the freedom to discover and develop this uniqueness.

As we have indicated previously, the true function of a child's education should be the process of helping him to discover his uniqueness, aiding him toward its development, and teaching him how to share it with others. Rather, education is an "imposition" of what is called "reality" upon the child. Society, on the other hand, should be the agent through which his uniqueness is shared, for it is in dire need of fresh, new approaches to individual and group living. But society has the idea that what has been for centuries, even if it has not proven true, is the best way. This fallacy, if adhered to, leads individuality to its doom.

Each child offers a new hope for the world. But this thought apparently frightens most people. What would society be like made up of all "individuals?" Would it not be unruly and lead to anarchy? We recoil in horror at this thought. We feel more comfortable with a "silent majority." We distrust and suspect "oddballs." The family must make the child "fit" into the societal scheme of things. Education is afforded a similar role. It is most successful when it maintains the status quo, when it makes what we call "good citizens." The definition of a "good citizen" is usually one who "thinks, behaves and responds like everyone else." Educators also feel that there is an essential body of knowledge which it is their duty to implant in each child. Their defense of this is that they are teaching "the wisdom of the ages."

To love oneself is to struggle to rediscover and maintain your uniqueness. It is understanding and appreciating the idea that you will be the only you to ever live upon this earth, that when you die so will all of your fantastic possibilities. It is the realization that even you are not totally aware of the wonders which lie dormant within yourself. Herbert Otto says only about 5 percent of our human potential is realized in our lifetime. Margaret Mead has hypothesized that 4 percent is discovered. What of the other 95 percent?

The psychiatrist R.D. Laing, has written: "We think much less than what we know, we know much less than what we love, we love much less than what there is, and to this precise extent we are much less than what we are!"

To Love Others You Must First Love Yourself

There is a you, lying dormant. A potential within you to be realized. It does not matter whether you have an intelligence quotient of 60 or 160, there is more of you than what you are presently aware of. Perhaps the only peace and joy in life lies in the pursuit of and the development of this potential. It's doubtful that one will realize all of his "self" in a lifetime even if his every moment were dedicated to it.

Goethe has Faust discover this when he says, "If on this earth one moment of peace could I find, then unto that moment would I say, 'Linger awhile, so fair thou art.' " If he rests from his searches even for a brief moment, he is courting the devil, for there can be no peace in man's struggle to become. The Gospel of St. John tells us that our house has many rooms, each with its own wonders to disclose. How can we be content to let spiders, rats, decay and death take over our house?

What may be is always potential for discovery. It's never too late. This knowledge should give man his greatest challenge — the pursuit of self — his own personal Odyssey; discovering his rooms and putting them in order. It should challenge him not only to be a good person, a loving person, a feeling person, an intelligent person, but the best, most loving, feeling, intelligent person he is capable of. His search is not in competition with anyone else's. He becomes his own personal challenge.

Love and the self are one and the discovery of either is the realization of both.

So loving yourself involves the discovery of the true wonder of you; not only the present you, but the many possibilities of you. It involves the continual realization that you are unique, like no other person in the world, that life is, or should be, the discovery, the development and the sharing of this uniqueness. The process is not always easy, for one is bound to find those who will feel threatened by a changing, growing you. But it will always be exciting, always be fresh and like all things new and changing, never be dull. The trip into oneself is the grandest, most enjoyable and longest lasting. The fare is cheap; it merely involves continual experiencing, evaluating, educating, trying out of new behavior. Only you can be the final judge in determining what is right for you.

The Western culture has been a culture of competitors. The worth of a man has always been measured by how much more he has than other men. If he has a larger home, a more powerful car, a more impressive formal education, he must be a better man. But these are not universal values. There are cultures whose highest adulation goes to the holy man, the teacher, who has spent his lifetime in self-discovery and has nothing of monetary value to show for it. There are cultures who value joy and peace of mind over property and busyness. They hypothesize that since all men must die, whether poor or rich, the only real goal of life is

*When man has love he is no longer
at the mercy of forces greater than
himself, for he, himself, becomes
the powerful force.*

the present joy and the realization of self in joy, not the collection of material things. There are areas where nature has taught and continues to teach this lesson with a vengeance. What good is accumulating objects or building large villas at the base of Mt. Etna? What is the purpose of permanent housing where monsoons come annually and wash away all but the people and the land?

The Thirties in the United States caused many to take a deep look at values. After the Market crash, men who had put their store in "things" went under with them, even to suicide. Other men, who had put their hope in themselves, sighed, "I did it once. I can do it again," and went out to create anew. Loving yourself involves appreciating the value of you above all things.

Loving yourself also involves the knowledge that only you can be you. If you try to be like anyone else, you may come very close, but you will always be second best. But, you are the best you. It is the easiest, most practical, most rewarding thing to be. Then it makes sense that you can only be to others what you are to yourself.

If you know, accept and appreciate yourself and your uniqueness, you will permit others to do so. If you value and appreciate the discovery of yourself, you will encourage others to engage in self-discovery. If you recognize your need to be free to discover who you are, you will allow others their freedom to do so, also. When you realize you are the best you, you will accept the fact that others are the best they. But it follows that it all starts with you. To the extent to which you know yourself, and we are all more alike than different, you can know others. When you love yourself, you will love others. And to the depth and extent to which you can love yourself, only to that depth and extent will you be able to love others.

TO LOVE
YOU MUST FREE
YOURSELF OF
LABELS

"Man has a pretty static picture of the world, accidentally or forcibly imprinted upon him by means of chains of conditioned associations. Man believes his imprint board is reality."

— *Timothy Leary.*

VII.

In a previous section we discussed the import of words in the process of learning to love. We mentioned that words caused a permanent imprint, a freezing of reality, through which all future learning and perception would then be filtered. This filtering is a great hindrance to love. If your learning has caused an avoidance reaction to black men or Jews or the Mexican, or those with different manners from yours, a different dress, then your possibilities of loving these human beings will be minimized.

LOVE

Man created words to free himself. He created language so that he could communicate himself to others and allow them to do the same. He intended words to help organize and record the wisdom of the past and dreams of the future. He found that words helped him in organizing his environment. But most of all, he used words to think with and to create. He developed language to free himself, never imagining that he would become a slave to language. He found that the very same labels he originated to merely stand for something soon had the power to become the thing itself. Man began to act as if the word was the thing. With names in hand, man assumed he had the 'thing' in hand. He inferred, therefore, that he could communicate it to others simply by using the label. When he discussed a Frenchman, he supposed that all people had the same static picture of a Frenchman as he. This, of course, was not so and thus his ability to communicate began to break down. The label tricked man into becoming its slave and distanced him from other human beings. He never stopped to ask what he or others actually understood about another individual when he labeled him "Communist," "Catholic," "Republican," "Jew." He did not bother to ask if the "communist" was also a good father, a gentle man, a dedicated teacher, a good human being, a warm lover, a pacifist, a dreamer or a creator. The negative stimuli produced by the word, "communist," were enough to convince him he could "hate" the individual. So it went.

When I was a child, it was popular to call Italians "Dagos" and "Wops." We moved into a neighborhood which had never had an Italian family living among them. Immediately the label went to work. "Dagos are all members of the Mafia." "A Dago in the neighborhood will cause property values to go down." "The peace of the neighborhood is gone. Dagos are such boisterous, emotional people."

For months we were ignored, though we tried to break down the barriers. We had been pushed aside, categorized. The connotation toward "Dagos" caused our neighbors to believe they knew us and be comfortable in rejecting us.

What they didn't know about us was far greater and more significant than what they did know. They didn't know that mama was a singer and our house was always full of music.

Mama, too, had great secret medical knowledge and while she was our physician none of the family was ever sick. Her treatments consisted mainly of two major remedies; "garlic," which was a general cure-all for daily use, and "polenta," which was a scalding hot, thick mixture of corn flour and water, placed steaming hot on our chests when all else failed. The garlic was tied, rubbed and raw, in a small handkerchief around our necks each morning before school. Strangely enough, we were never ill.

(I have developed a theory about this. With raw garlic on us, no one ever got close enough to pass on germs.) The polenta worked miracles, too, though I've never been able to figure out what pharmaceutical value it had. Perhaps it was the realization of the fact that whatever illness was present was minor compared to the second degree burns left by the steaming hot corn meal on our skin. These were already reason enough for neighbors not to exclude us. What better medical remedies could have been shared? What arias and operas will they never again have the opportunity to hear so superbly performed?

Papa made wine which was fit for a Papal altar. He also demanded continual growth in the education of all of us. His favorite question, asked of each of us after every meal, was "Well, what new thing did you learn today?" He was always eager to learn and continually concerned about his own education. We thought the wine superb. In fact, I was weaned on it. The practice of sharing new knowledge was not as appealing. When he was with us for dinner, the family was busy going through the encyclopedia looking for something new to teach papa, while he sat back, curled his moustache and sipped his wine. Our exclusive neighbors were missing this intellectual exchange and above all, the palatal delights of home-made "vino rosso."

To be able to love one must control his linguistic

environment, "defrost" all preconceived notions brought on by old word traps. Buckminster Fuller is said to have been so concerned with his being controlled by words that he spent two years, mostly alone, studying what words meant specifically to him. Only after a two-year period did he feel sufficiently free from language traps to use language as an agent for bringing things closer rather than pushing them away, for making language his tool.

The effect of language on personality is now the science of psycholinguistics. The psycholinguist is repeatedly showing how language affects behavior. There are those who have created a positive linguistic environment. Their words are joyful, pleasant, reflective of the beautiful, reinforcing of the good. Others are controlled by negative words. Their lives are made up of callous words, caustic, lifeless, dreary, tedious, depressing words, devoid of joy, unpleasant, reinforcing of the negative.

Perhaps the most positive word in the English language and that most conducive to continued growth in love is "Yes." "Yes" is the best "defroster" of frozen symbols and ideas. A lover says "Yes" to life, "Yes" to joy, "Yes" to knowledge, "Yes" to people, "Yes" to differences. He realizes that all things and people have something to offer him, that all things are in all things. If "Yes" is too threatening, he tries "Maybe."

If one wishes to be a lover he must start by saying 'YES' to love.

To Love You Must Free Yourself Of Labels

To say "No" to something, is to exclude it; to exclude it is to close it out, perhaps forever.

James Joyce, in his masterpiece, *Ulysses*, ends the book with the greatest affirmation in literature when he has Molly sigh several pages of "Yesses." "Yes. Yes. Yes. Yes!"

Dag Hammarskjold wrote in his fantastically personal *Markings*, "I don't know who — or what — put the question, I don't know when it was put. I don't even remember answering. But at some moment I did answer "Yes" to Someone or something. And from that hour I was certain that existence is meaningful and that, therefore, my life, in self-surrender, had a goal."

If one wishes to be a lover, he must start by saying "Yes" to love. He can do this by looking carefully and coolly at the words he uses when he talks to his wife and children, to his boss and co-workers, to his neighbors and close friends, to his salesgirl and the gas station attendant.

For the words you use will tell you what you are, what you have seen, what you have learned and how you have learned it. For you are your words and they can be a long and important step on the road to discovery of love.

LOVE
INVOLVES
RESPONSIBILITY

"*Only when it is a duty to love, only then is love eternally and happily secured against despair.*"

—*Kierkegaard.*

VIII.

Before man can love all men or any man, his first
responsibility in love is, and always will be, to himself. The Gospel statement, "You shall love your
neighbor as yourself," presupposes self-love and suggests that man "shall" love others to the extent to
which he loves himself. We have already discussed
this love of self in a previous section, so we shall
not belabor the fact. Suffice it to say that only to
the depth and the extent to which one feels responsibility to grow in self love, so can he feel this
toward helping others to do so. All men are re-

lated to a greater or smaller extent, interconnected, and each man who comes closer to himself in any way comes closer to others.

Albert Schweitzer said repeatedly that as long as there was a man in the world who was hungry, sick, lonely or living in fear, he was his responsibility. He affirmed this by living a life in this belief; a life of the loftiest order, the highest fulfillment, the greatest joy, the most elevated dignity and, therefore, the most towering love.

Society has not produced many Schweitzers, but all of us know and accept some level of responsibility to ourselves and to others. The fact is, to be human is to be responsible.

Many men find it difficult to assume full responsibility for even themselves, let alone for another individual, or a group of individuals. Therefore, the idea of being accountable for a "family of man" seems to them inconceivable, unrealistic, idealistic nonsense.

When love is truly responsible, it is one's duty to love all men. Man has no choice but to accept this duty, for when he does not, he finds his alternatives lie in loneliness, destruction and despair. To assume this responsibility is for him to become involved in delight in mystery and in growth. It is to dedicate himself to the process of helping others to realize their love through him. Simply speaking, to be responsible in love is to help other men to love. To be helped toward realizing your love is to be loved by other men.

Men have been known to approach this responsibility to love from different means, but the ends are always the same, universal love. Some begin with a deep personal involvement with another individual. From this, they learn that love cannot be exclusive. They learn that if love is to grow, it will need diverse minds, innumerable individuals, and the exploration of varied paths. No one human being can afford him all of these things, so he must enlarge his love to include all mankind in his love. The more all encompassing his love, the greater his growth. The love of humanity is the natural outgrowth of love for a single individual. From one man to all men.

Herbert Otto states: "Only in a continuing relationship is there a possibility for love to become deeper and fuller so that it envelops all of our life and extends into the community." For only a deep relationship offers "the adventure of uncovering the depth of our love, the height of our humanity. It means risking ourselves physically and emotionally; leaving old habit patterns and developing new ones; being able to express our desires fully, while sensitive to the needs of the other; being aware that each changes at his own rate, and unafraid to ask for help when needed."

Others have felt that anything less than love of all men is not love at all. They argue that who does not love all men sincerely cannot love even a single person deeply, since all men are one. Loving all men is the same as loving each man.

Kierkegaard is one of the chief proponents of this idea. He says, "It is, in fact, Christian love which discovers and knows that one's neighbor exists and that . . . it is one and the same thing . . . everyone is one's neighbor. If it were not a duty to love, then, there would be no concept of neighbor at all. But only when one loves his neighbor, only then is the selfishness of preferential love rooted out and the equality of the eternal preserved."

In dedicating himself to humanity, Schweitzer, on the one hand, finds it to be only an extension of the love he felt for each living thing. Through loving a single person, Herbert Otto feels that one acquires enough strength to assume the responsibility for the community of man. No matter which way it is approached, one finds that love is not selfish and exclusive, but selfless and inclusive. The fact remains that the world still finds it difficult to accept universal truth. If one loves only himself, he's labeled egocentric, self-centered and selfish. If he loves himself and a small community, including a wife and family in his love, society will call him a true lover and praise him as a sound man. But, if he loves all men in an extremely high-minded manner, he's often ridiculed by the world as naive, fanciful and foolish.

The third responsibility love implies lies in the

continued assurance that it will always be directed in growth, personal growth as well as the growth of selves and those whom we love.

Antoine Saint-Exupery has defined love as "the process of my leading you back to yourself." In this statement, he is confirming his faith in man's ability to guide another to love. He suggests that a growing Self brings with it a growing love.

Love abhors waste, especially waste of human potential.

At a recent wedding ceremony where two young people were permitted to write their own marriage vows, they repeated, "I will love you as long as I can help you grow in love." This, it seems to me, is the essence of loving another, to assure them that we are dedicated to their growth, to the actualization of their limitless potential. This couple was determined to use their united energies in helping each other through the endless process of discovering who they really are, then revel forever in this continually changing knowledge and discovery. It is only in this way that human love can flourish. As soon as the love relationship does not lead me to me, as soon as I in a love relationship do not lead another person to himself, this love, even if it seems to be the most secure and ecstatic attachment I have ever experienced, is not true love. For real love is dedicated to a continual becoming. When, for any reason, this process ceases, love becomes tedious,

As soon as the love relationship does not lead me to me, As soon as I, in a love relationship, do not lead the other person to himself, this love, even if it seems to be the most secure and ecstatic attachment I have ever experienced, is not true love.

listless and is doomed to fade. It decays. It destroys itself. So, what may seem like a beginning is, in actuality, only the beginning of an end.

Responsibility of any kind can seem intimidating and for this reason man may often be afraid of truly deep relationships with other human beings. A relationship suggests to him the most extreme of responsibilities. It implies a burden, a restriction to his freedom, seldom the converse. A student in love class, for instance, commented, "I've always been afraid of a deep relationship because of the responsibility it seemed to impose. I was afraid of the demands it would make of me and I worried that I wouldn't be able to meet those demands. I was amazed to find that when I did get the courage to form a relationship, I actually became stronger. I acquired two minds instead of one, four hands, four arms, four legs, and another's world. In joining forces with someone, I got twice the strength to grow, with twice as many alternatives. Now, it's easier for me to love others. I am stronger and I am less afraid." He had discovered an important insight.

Another responsibility of love is to create joy. Joy is always an integral part of loving. There is joy in every act of life, no matter how menial or repetitive. To work in love is to work in joy. To live in love is to live in joy. You may not have before you the most creative and satisfying day to live, but you know that live it you must. You can make the day a chore; dull, nerve-wracking, frustrating, a waste of time. Or the same day can be taken on with energy, enthusiasm and a determination to make it one of the best days of your life, for yourself and those about you. To live each moment as if, as the popular saying goes, "it is the last day of your life." It is the same day, requiring the same energy and hours. The difference is that you can choose to live it with joy or live it in misery. Why not choose joy?

In one of my classes I ask my students to write on the subject, "If I were to die tomorrow, how would I live tonight?" Answering this question always brings great insight. In working on this exercise students find that in so many ways they are wasting time, precious time. That though, in their youth, death is far off, even for the longest lived of all, time of life is limited. Why not live it in joy?

Responsible love needs expression. Love is communication. As man must assume the responsibility for expressing his joy, in like manner he is responsible for letting his sorrow and loneliness be known. In reality, it seems the more devastated one becomes, the more he builds defenses, rationalizations, and creates walls behind which to grumble. He is misunderstood. He is unloved. He is abused. He is exploited. In other words, the more he seems to need loving understanding, the more he moves away from any possibility of receiving it. The "pouting syndrome" is the perfect example of this. If one needs, one must let others know of his need or it can never be met. Even lovers are not mind readers. Oftentimes, when people have allowed themselves to express a need, they are surprised at the response they have received. For example, "I had no idea you were lonely." "You always seemed so self-sufficient, so composed, so fulfilled. I'm really pleased to know you're human." As one shows others he loves them, so must he reveal to them his need for love. You cannot assume that people, even those most close to you, will know and understand your unexpressed needs and feelings. If you want people to know you, you are responsible for communicating yourself to them.

Responsible love is accepting and understanding. Love grows at different rates and in different directions in all individuals. Love in marriage, or any close relationship, for example, is the process of growing hand in hand, but separately. Separately, because it's impossible to expect that two individuals, even in love, will grow at the same rate and in the same direction. This means that one may not always totally understand or appreciate another's growth or its resultant behavior. But love helps us to accept the fact that the other individual is behaving only as he is able to behave at the moment. To ask that he act otherwise is to ask the impossible.

LOVE

Responsible love is empathic. The word, empathy, though perhaps overused, is still a great word. It means to "feel" with. It does not imply "total understanding." We know that we can never really understand another person, but since in love we have so many positive and common elements, there is hope. If behavior is contradictory to our expectations or annoying or a disappointment to us, it must be seen as merely a passing phase. Love is always changing and always learning. Love offers the greatest flexibility. It asks only that we accept behavior as it is expressed in the knowledge that this behavior is not permanent. It is not a matter of forgiving. Forgiving, in a sense, is condescending. It is a matter of accepting the person unconditionally for what he is at the moment, realizing that what he is today is not what he will be tomorrow. A lover is, then, constantly watching, listening, waiting, feeling, adjusting, readjusting and changing.

If two people grow apart in love, it is usually due to the fact that one or the other refuses to grow or change. In this case, a lover can either decide to adjust to the behavior, ignore it or, after all else seems useless, move away from it, and leave. You may ask the question, "But is 'moving away' really love?" Indeed, it is. For if a lover stands in the way of another then he is no longer loving.

Responsible love has at its universal core man's humanity. In the deepest sense, we all have a core of humanness. The greatest thing a man can be is a human being with the strengths and the frailities implied in the meaning. The world's greatest figures have often been the most "human" and have been the least reticent to reveal it. On earth, Jesus wept, felt loneliness, disappointment, pain and despair. Only in this way could he understand what it was to be a man. Buddha knew the most basic human characteristics; confusion, egocentricity, pride, envy, even indigestion. Gandhi felt humility, exhaustion, physical deprivation, illness, frailty, torture, and suffered from what he called the "temporal accident of his own personality." In varying degrees we have all felt what great men such as Jesus, Buddha, and Gandhi felt. To that degree we have empathy with them — a common tie.

We have often heard or said to ourselves, "It's only human." We say this because we know that perfection is a concept that for most of us is far off. In the meantime, we must make do with what we have. But it is simple to understand that it is no more easy for the father in India to stand by and watch his family starve than it would be for a father anywhere in the world. The Africans are just as capable of happiness as are the Peruvians. The wealthy are just as susceptible to tears as are the poor. The wise are just as capable of being confused as the retarded. In other words, it is the hu-

Man has no choice but to love.
For when he does not, he finds his
alternatives lie in loneliness,
destruction and despair.

manity of man that gives us the common base from which we can have empathy in love.

It's the empathy that makes us responsible in love to all men. With each man who dies in the world, each of us dies a little. With each person who suffers, we, too, suffer a little. With each child born in the world, we all become richer in possibilities. We're all unconditionally like the other; it is just that we are in diverse lands, playing different roles in a variety of robes before dissimilar backdrops on various stages before foreign audiences. It would be interesting if we could often change robes and stand on many stages in our lifetime. It would give us great insight into man's universality. We exist for each individual as each individual exists for us all.

If all men were naked and we were asked to shut our eyes and feel, the flowergirl could be confused with the queen, the jester could pass as king, and the president could be taken as the migrant worker or the angry militant. There is perhaps no greater knowledge than this, that each person in the world, no matter how lowly or how princely, is basically a human being. To turn anyone out will be to lose all the possibilities offered through the intimacy of knowing deeply and feeling sincerely with another.

Responsible love shares. In actuality, no man possesses anything but himself. The saying that "you can't take it with you," though overused, is singularly a true one. One can hold on to nothing or no one. Love shares with others. What purpose of knowledge if it isn't offered to students? What meaning has beauty that isn't presented for all to experience? What good is love that isn't freely given? Love is always an active sharing. If one has love to give, he may impart it to all in the world and he will still have the same love he started with. We never lose anything by sharing it, for nothing is ever solely ours to start with. In fact, love acquires meaning only as it's shared.

An interesting experiment was performed in a sociology class at an eastern American college. The professor was discussing the process of giving and how it relates to responsibility. He asked the class to give ten cents to any of the following three needy situations. First, there was a very severe drought in Southern India for which money was needed. Women and children were dying; men were despondent. By giving they would be helping in a battle for life itself. Secondly, they could offer their ten cents toward a college fund being organized to help an excellent black student. The student was being forced to leave school due to an insurmountable family misfortune which could only be remedied with instant cash. Thirdly, they could contribute to a fund being started to purchase a new Xerox machine for student use. This machine would most assuredly make their academic life much easier. The results of the lesson will not be a surprise to many and a great shock to a few. Over 85 percent of the students, by secret ballot, donated their ten cents toward the purchase of the Xerox machine for their own immediate use. The next larger amount, about 12 percent, was given for the black student to remain in school. Only 3 percent of the students gave to the most urgent need, to maintain life in India.

The further away the problem the less was the responsibility to share felt. The need or the urgency of the need did not seem to matter. It was not the selfless "I" but the selfish "I" that lost the opportunity to give life to the Indian or education to the black man. It was the selfish "I" who ignored the fact that in the end he had gained little. Do all the Xerox machines in the world have the worth of a single life? To not realize this is to place value upon empty "things," which when death pays its inevitable call, will only have to be surrendered at its door.

Lastly, responsible love rises even beyond hope. The ability to hope, certainly, is one of the greatest lifesaving phenomena of man. In hope, man shows a deep respect and faith in man's ability to change, a belief in "the integrity of the universe," in new beginnings, in exciting tomorrows. Hope is essential to man, for man is not yet brave enough to exist without it. To live without hope would be devastating for him. Man has not yet learned to work for the joy of work, learn for the sake of growth, create for the expression and the exaltation in the act, or to love simply for the pleasure of loving; he still requires a reward. Until man learns to do these things, hope will have to be his basic motivating force. In work, he'll require more wages and better titles; in knowledge, he'll require degrees and diplomas; in creativity, he'll require recognition; in love, he'll require assurance. Until he appreciates that each of these are their own reward, he'll need hope as his crutch. There is nothing wrong with hope in love; it is simply the second best thing.

In the meantime, hope is admittedly a powerful creative force. For, as Norman Cousins has put it, "Hope is the beginning of plans. It gives men a destination, a sense of direction for getting there, and the energy to get started. It enlarges sensitivities. It gives proper values to feelings as well as to facts." His hope involves "a rekindling of human imagination — about life as man might like it; about the full use of his intelligence to bring sanity and sensitivity to his world and to his art; about the importance of the individual; about his capacity for creating new institutions, discovering new approaches, sensing new possibilities."

Certainly, all this is true. But love goes beyond hope. Hope is a beginning. Love is forever.

LOVE
RECOGNIZES
NEEDS

"*A mind not to be changed by place or time, the mind is its own place, and in itself can make a Heaven of Hell, a Hell of Heaven.*"
—*John Milton.*

IX.

Man has both physical and emotional needs. His physical needs, though he spends most of his time — indeed, most of his life — meeting them, are the simplest to satisfy. Man requires but a small quantity of food — most of us eat far too much — some shelter from the elements — we hardly need the large homes we live in — clothing in winter — many still use a fig leaf in parts of the world — and, of course, nurturing and water. Everything beyond this is luxury, fine to have, of course, for comfort's sake, but not necessary for his survival. Two-thirds of today's world attest to this.

LOVE

But man has other needs as well: emotional needs. These, too, are few, but every bit as important as his physical requirements, yet not so simple. If they aren't met, they can be as devastating as physical hunger, as uncomfortable as lack of shelter, as incapacitating as thirst. The frustration, isolation and anxiety brought about by unmet emotional needs can, like physical privation, produce death or a degree of living death — neurosis and psychosis.

Still, aware of this, man continues to spend only a small portion of his time in the activities involved in meeting his emotional needs and in the process of aiding others toward the satisfaction of their needs. Certainly, there are few people who would consider their emotional needs important enough to warrant the equal time spent earning the wages with which their physical necessities are satisfied.

Man's basic psychological needs are these. He requires to be seen, recognized, appreciated, heard, fondled, sexually satisfied. He must be allowed the freedom to choose his own way, to grow at his own rate and to make his own mistakes, to learn. He needs to accept himself and other human beings and be accepted by them. He desires to be an "I" as well as a "we." He strives to grow into the unique individual he is.

Love recognizes all these needs or it isn't love. If any are unmet, the individual can never be totally realized and will remain hidden, in part, even from

imself. It is much like a tree, certain branches of
which have been kept from the sun while the re-
mainder of the tree grows; the parts which have
been deprived of sunshine will never develop in the
normal way.

The bank president, for example, may be a
highly efficient, intelligent, accepted, respected,
contributing member of the community. In all
ways, it seems, he's like the strong growing tree.
But his wife knows that when it comes to eating
habits he has the limited tastes of a child, and in the
bedroom, he is as impotent as one. Somewhere
along in his emotional growth, he needed. The needs
were unmet. In order to continue to grow, he put
the need aside — psychologically speaking — and
his eating and sexual habits remained at a childish
level while the rest of him went on toward ma-
turity. Of course, this is an oversimplification of the
dynamics involved, which are far more complex
and subtle. But the main point I wish to make here
is the fact that man will suffer for unmet needs.

Man has a need to be seen, heard and fondled.
Love recognizes these needs. Each individual seems
to be far too busy these days to stop and look at or
listen to anyone, even his own family. This, I call
the "invisible man" syndrome. One is directly before you each day, at meals, in the living room, even
in bed. You know he's there, but you don't see him,
you don't look at him.

LOVE

If you love someone, you'll look at him carefully. He is changing each day through a beautiful, gradual process which you will surely miss if you do not learn to watch. When is the last time you looked at your wife or husband's face, your child's face, your mother's face? For that matter, how long has it been since you looked deeply at yourself, not while shaving or washing or putting on eye shadow, but at a moment of peace, just looking?

The American black man has known this feeling of being invisible for years. So much so that he has called himself the "Invisible Man." The existentialist has formed a whole philosophy around the idea of the futility of man's personal struggle for recognition, for his search for affirmation of his real existence and the meaning of that existence. A lover recognizes the need of others to be seen. He looks.

Man needs just as surely to be heard. I refer to the lack of this as the "cocktail party" syndrome. Here there are great mobs of people all gaily chatting *at* one another, exchanging what has been called "small talk." Much is spoken, but little is heard or listened to. It might be said that it is merely the setting of air into vibration — vibration does not become sound until it's picked up by the ear and the vibrations are translated and interpreted into symbols by the brain. The brain plays little part at the usual cocktail party except as an organ to be numbed.

Even when one person does listen to another, he

often hears what he wishes to hear. He has a capacity to choose or screen out what is uncomfortable for him.

In an interesting book by Alexandra David-Neel and Lama Yongden, *The Secret Oral Teachings in Tibetan Buddhist Sects*, the author tells how she approached a learned Tibetan regarding her plan to write the book. The wise man's answer is both amusing and illustrative of the point I am trying to make. He says: "Waste of time. The great majority of readers and hearers are the same all over the world. I have no doubt that the people in your country are like those I have met in China and India, and these latter were just like Tibetans. If you speak to them of profound truths they yawn, and, if they dare, they leave you but if you tell them absurd fables they are all eyes and ears. They wish the doctrines preached to them, whether religious, philosophic, or social, to be agreeable, to be consistent with their conceptions, to satisfy their inclinations, in fact that they find themselves in them, and that they feel themselves approved by them."

To add to the confusion, words often mean different things to different people. This sometimes produces a rather strange phenomenon which Timothy Leary has referred to as "my Checkerboard trying to communicate with your Monopoly game." This scene has been beautifully portrayed by Edward Albee in *The American Dream*, which opens with such a conversation between a man and his wife; she discussing in minute detail a shopping episode, he a thousand miles away in his own thoughts. Her only punctuation marks are when she stops long enough to ask him to repeat what she has said. She wants to be certain he has heard. To be sure, he has not "heard" a word, but he repeats it perfectly. The audiences find the scene hilarious. Strange that they don't weep, since most of us find ourselves in this play each day of our lives. Perhaps if we listened to another person, truly listened, we could hear his joy or his cry. Love listens. Love hears.

Love touches, fondles. Physical love is necessary for happiness, growth and development. We have mentioned earlier that the infant needs to be fondled or he will die even if all his biological needs are met. Freud's statement that at the base of all mental illness is the lack of sensual gratification has had many and varied interpretations, even to labeling him a "dirty old man." What he meant by sensual gratification extended from the mother nursing her child and changing his diapers to the most passionate of sexual experiences, and all physical gradations in between. Even a handshake may be classified as sensual gratification. No matter the degree, and we will hope that all men will take the opportunity to experience the entire gamut of experience, man needs to be touched. The power of the sexual drive attests to this. In some people it becomes so powerful that it directs their entire lives. Kingdoms have been known to rise and fall, wars have been declared, murders have been committed just so that someone could have that moment of sexual union; often without love in the real sense, strictly in passion.

Love is not sex, though sensual gratification in varying degrees is always a part of love. To attempt to write a book on love without the consideration of the import of sex would be absurd. It is impossible to realize a situation where one loves deeply and sincerely without a desire for some form of sensual gratification. Our mores against the most superficial human contact are so great, even to laws which prohibit it, that many have moved almost completely away from any form of physical love except on a purely animalistic level. Even the choice of shaking hands, man with woman, is, according to Emily Post, at the discretion of the woman. If she extends her hand, the male accepts it. But she is also "right" not to extend it. And so we distance ourselves from each other, through manners as well as laws.

There is no doubt that someone is real when you touch them, when you feel their flesh on yours, even for a brief moment. I continually breach etiquette in that I always extend my hand to men and women alike; I cause looks of horror when I hold their hand longer than is accepted and cover it

In love, each man is his own
personal challenge.

warmly with my free hand. It frightens some —
who look at me quizzically wondering, "What is he
after?" — but it mostly affirms to us both that we
are two human beings relating on a very real level.
It might present a new philosophical statement:
"We touch, therefore we are." Surely there are
few people who do not find being touched or
touching others pleasurable. There are some, of
course, who find it, in a pathological way, unpleasant. I have known occasions when people
have said, "Please don't touch me. I prefer not being
touched." Of course, it is their right, which must
be respected. Nevertheless, love is physical, it
touches.

Love needs freedom. We discussed earlier that, in
every sense, love is always free. It is both given and
received freely, but it also needs freedom in order to
grow. Each man growing in love will find his own
way, his own path to love. We cannot force others
into our way; we can only encourage them to find
their own. Carlos Casteneda in his startlingly interesting book on the Yaqui Indians, *The Teachings
of Don Juan*, quotes Don Juan's wisdom: "You
must always keep in mind that a path is only a path;
if you feel you must not follow it, you must not
stay with it under any circumstances . . . any path
is only a path, there is no affront to yourself or
others in dropping it if that is what your head tells
you to do. But your decision to keep on the path or

to leave it must be free of fear or ambition. I warn
you! Look at every path closely and deliberately.
Try it as many times as you think necessary. Then
ask ourself, and you alone, one question . . . It is
this . . . Does this path have a heart? All paths are
the same; they lead nowhere. They are paths going through the brush, or into the brush. Does this
path have a heart is the question. If it does, then the
path is good; if it doesn't, it is of no use. Both paths
lead nowhere, but one has heart and the other
doesn't. One makes for a joyful journey; as long as
you follow it you will be one with it. The other will
make you curse your life. One makes you strong,
the other weakens you."

Each individual can judge for himself alone which
path has heart for him. Where paths cross there is
union; where they run parallel there is peace, pro-
vided that each path loves and honors the other.

Love never gives direction, for it knows that to
lead a man off his path is to give him our path which
will never be truly right for him and is certain to
"weaken" him. He must be free to go his own way,
in his chosen manner and at his special rate. He
must be free to make his own mistakes and learn
from them what he can. Our love is there to give
him sustenance, the strength to continue his seeking
securely, in joy, and offer him the day-by-day encouragement he will require. Any aid we give is
only directed in helping him to find the self which

184

he has long since been seeking. Love is his guide, not his leader. Each man is his own leader. Love never reflects the giver. For if there is any detection of our aid, then we have kept the loved one from truly traveling his own path and he has not been really free. He has his path and love encourages him on his way, even if his path does not intersect with our desired path. To hold him to what we believe to be the right path for him is to lead him into darkness and as Thoreau says, "Birds never sing in caves."

Love listens to its own needs. Society is replete with rules, regulations and guidelines to finding love and social acceptance. Often, man is so taken up with what others believe or will think or say, that he stops listening to what *he* believes, thinks or says. Society will tell him that he must live in a certain type of house. He, on the other had, has always wanted to live in a modified igloo. If he builds an igloo, "people" will think him mad, so he builds a ranch-style house which drives "him" mad. He likes his walls a warm color, orange perhaps. He has always loved orange, even as a child. But the interior decorator tells him that "no one paints walls orange," that avocado green is delightful and very "in." So, he has his walls painted green and takes the decorator's advice to add purple drapes — "very smart" — and a puce rug — "the latest thing." So he has green walls, purple curtains and a puce rug. Each time he walks into the room he becomes physically ill, but the neighbors and "Better Homes & Gardens" approve, so it must be right. Homes are built for contractors, clothes are designed by sadistic couturiers, beauty is defined by Hollywood and Cinecitta and the individual is lost. He becomes all the things others dictate, sometimes without being consciously aware of it.

We are caught up in trivia, all of which we are told certainly will bring us love. Each day it becomes more and more impossible for us to emerge from the bathroom. We rise; we exercise for twenty minutes; then, we shower, dry ourselves, use powders or creams for our skin, brush our teeth using a mouthwash to be "doubly sure," brush our hair two hundred times after we have shampooed it, conditioned it, dried it, set it and combed it. We deodorize ourselves, bind ourselves into clothes, push our feet into shoes, make our bed, grab a cup of coffee and we are ready for the day. With some, the same routine is repeated before bed each night, only in reverse. As a result, we no longer know what a human being smells like and are repelled by natural human odors. We are so clean that we have little or no resistance against germs when we travel outside our own country. We are so involved in what must be done that we have no time to do what we will to do. I am not advocating a return to poor hygiene, the mass murder of all those who write books of etiquette that so complicate our lives, or the exile of all clothes designers and interior decorators and advertisers. I am simply suggesting that man must listen to his own "drummer" or he will be marched right out of himself.

Love listens to its own needs and appreciates its own uniqueness. It abhors the fact that men are becoming more and more the same, so that it will not be long before the only way he will be identifiable as an individual will be through his social security number.

Love, then, recognizes needs, physical and emotional. It sees as well as looks, listens as well as hears. Love touches, fondles and revels in sensual gratification. Love is free and cannot be realized unless it is left free. Love finds its own path, sets its own pace and travels in its own way. Love recognizes and appreciates its uniqueness. Love needs no recognition, for if its effect is recognizable, it is not true love at all.

LOVE
REQUIRES ONE
TO BE STRONG

"It is the weak who are cruel. Gentleness can only be expected from the strong."
—Leo Rosten.)

X.

To live in love is life's greatest challenge. It requires more subtlety, flexibility, sensitivity, understanding, acceptance, tolerance, knowledge and strength than any other human endeavor or emotion, for love and the actual world make up what seem like two great contradictory forces. On the one hand, man may know that only by being vulnerable can he truly offer and accept love. At the same time, he knows that if he reveals this vulnerability in daily life he often runs the risk of being misused, taken advantage of. He senses that if he holds a part of himself in reserve to protect this vulnerability, he will always receive in return only the partial love he gives. So, the only chance he has for a depth of love is to give all that he has. Yet, he discovers that when he gives all that he has, he is often left with little or nothing in return.

He knows he must trust and believe in love, for it's the only approach to love. Yet, if he expresses his trust and belief, society doesn't hesitate to abuse him and take him for a fool. If he has hope in love and knows that it's only with this hope that he can make the dream of an all-loving humanity a reality, society ridicules him as an idealistic dreamer. If he doesn't seek love frantically, he's suspected of being impotent and an "odd-ball." Yet, he knows that love isn't to be sought after, it's everywhere, and to search is self-deception, a charade. If he decides to spend each moment of his life, living in love, in the knowledge that he is most real and human when he is living love, society labels him a weak-minded romantic. Love and the practices of the real world seem at odds, miles apart. It is no wonder so many people do not have the courage to attempt to bridge the gap, for in practice, the gap seems unbridgeable. Man has, on the one hand, the understanding and drives for growing in love, but society makes this knowledge difficult in practice. Society's reality differs from love's reality. The strength to believe in love when you are pitted against a nonreinforcing proving ground is more than most people can accept. So they find it easier to put love aside, to reserve it for special people on unique occasions and join forces with society in questioning its supposed reality.

To be open to love, to trust and believe in love, to be hopeful in love and live in love, you need the greatest strength. This condition is so seldom experienced in real life that people don't know how to cope with it, even when they discover it. They crucify a Jesus, shoot a Gandhi, behead a Thomas More and poison a Socrates. Society has little place for honesty, tenderness, goodness or concern. These get in the way of the "way of the world." The phenomenon has been the basis for great works of literature from Plato's *Republic* and Dostoevsky's *The Idiot*, to Kazantzakis' *The Greek Passion* and Luis Bunuel's *The Nazarene*. It's almost like a game. People seek a figure to exhalt. They select him carefully, spend some time at his feet in adulation, then get great satisfaction in the slaughter. It's as if they cannot handle perfection, as if it causes them to reflect upon themselves, to move them to change, the thought of which is perhaps too uncomfortable and painful. It's easier not to see or concern themselves with perfection. Then they can be content with their own imperfection.

It's a fact that man does not move in a world of lovers. If he deals in the world of men, he's more likely to come upon selfishness, cruelty, deception, manipulation and like parasitic actions. If he depends upon the real world outside of himself for reinforcement, he'll be disillusioned and soon discovers that society and men are far less than perfect. For his society was created by less than perfect men. To cope with what he finds and to still live in love, he must have strength. He'll only survive if this strength lies within himself. He must not put his love upon the world and if it is rejected blame the world for its insensitivity. If he finds no love, he can blame only the fact that he has no love. He must have love securely in himself. He must dedicate himself to love, be resolute in his love and unwavering in his love. He must not be as Voltaire's foolish *Candide* and recognize only goodness even where evil exists. He must also know evil, hate and bigotry as real phenomena, but he must see love as the greater force. He must not doubt this even for a moment or he is lost. His only salvation is to dedicate himself to love, in the same fashion as Gandhi did to militant nonviolence, as Socrates did to truth, as Jesus did to love and as More did to integrity. Only then will he have the strength to combat the forces of doubt, confusion and contradiction. He can depend upon no one or no thing for reinforcement and assurance but *himself*. This may be a lonely path, but it's less lonely if he will understand the following:

Love Requires One To Be Strong

His main function is to help unfold his true
Self.

Equal to this function is helping others to
become strong, and perfect themselves
as unique individuals.

He will do this best by affording all persons the opportunity to show their
feelings, express their aspirations and
share their dreams.

He must see the forces labeled "evil" as
emanating from suffering people who,
like himself, are "human" and in the
process of attempting to perfect their
"beings."

He must combat these forces of evil through
an active love which is deeply concerned and interested in each person's
free quest for self-discovery.

He must believe that it is not the world that
is ugly, bitter and destructive, but it is
what man has done to the world that
makes it appear so.

He must be a model. Not a model of perfection, a state not often reached by man,
but a model human being. For being a
good human being is the greatest thing
he can be.

To live in love is life's greatest challenge.

He must be able to forgive himself for being less than perfect.

He must understand that change is inevitable, and that when it is directed in love and self-realization, it is always good.

He must be convinced that behavior, to be learned, must be tried out. "To be is to do."

He must learn that he cannot be loved by all men. That is the ideal. In the world of men, it is not often found. He can be the finest plum in the world, ripe, juicy, sweet, succulent and offer himself to all. But he must remember that there will be men who do not like plums.

He must understand that if he is the world's finest plum and someone he loves does not like plums, he has the choice of becoming a banana. But he must be warned that if he chooses to become a banana, he will be a second rate banana. But he can always be the best plum.

He must realize that if he chooses to be a second rate banana, he runs the risk of the loved one finding him second best and, wanting only the best, discarding him. He can then spend his life trying to become the best banana — which is impossible if he is a plum — or he can seek again to be the best plum.

He must endeavor to love all men even if he isn't loved by them. He doesn't love to be loved; he loves to love.

He must reject no man, for he realizes that he is a part of every man and to reject even one man, is to reject himself.

He must know that if he loves all men and is rejected by one, he must not pull away in fear, pain, disappointment or anger. It is not the other man's fault. He was not ready for what was offered. Love was not offered him with conditions. He gave love because he was fortunate enough to have it to give, because he felt joy in the giving, not for what he would receive in return.

He must understand that, if he is rejected in one love, there are hundreds of others awaiting love. The idea that there is but *one* right love is deception. There are *many* right loves.

These ideas will aid in giving you the strength to be a lover, for to be a lover will require that you continually have the subtlety of the very wise, the flexibility of the child, the sensitivity of the artist, the understanding of the philosopher, the acceptance of the saint, the tolerance of the dedicated, the knowledge of the scholar, and the fortitude of the certain. A tall order! All of these qualities will grow in him who chooses love for these are already a part of his potential and will be realized through loving. It becomes, then, a matter of loving your way to love.

LOVE
OFFERS
NO APOLOGY

"If I am level with the lowest, I am nothing; and if I did not know for a certainty that the craziest sot in the village is my equal, and were not proud to have him walk with me as my friend, I would not write another word—for this is my strength."
                                   —Edward Carpenter.

XI.

This short book has been no more than what was promised, hardly a deep philosophical or definitive work on love, nor a scholarly exploration of the phenomenon. This responsibility will have to be assumed by a man or woman far wiser, experienced, poetic and knowledgeable than I.

Rather, this work is and was intended to be a sharing. It is, in this sense, a work of love. If the message is received or not, it has been worth the effort, for in the writing a book on love, I have intentionally exposed myself to praise or ridicule,

"...and we ourselves shall be loved for a while and forgotten. But the love will have been enough; all those impulses of love return to the love that made them. Even memory is not necessary for love. There is a land of the living and a land of the dead, and the bridge is love, the only survival, the only meaning."

—*Thornton Wilder.*

acceptance or rejection; I have made myself totally vulnerable. Vulnerability is always at the heart of love.

Father William Du Bay stated it far better than I, when he said, "The most human thing we have to do in life is to learn to speak our honest convictions and feelings and live with the consequences. This is the first requirement of love, and it makes us vulnerable to other people who may ridicule us. But our vulnerability is the only thing we can give to other people."

Yes . . . !

LOVE

A Note about the Author

Leo Buscaglia, Ph.D., is Associate Professor of Education at the University of Southern California. Through his numerous lectures and appearances, Dr. Buscaglia, a native Californian, is universally known and loved.

Because of his awareness of life, he developed a "love" course at USC. *Love* is a result of the interactions with his students in this course. Dr. Buscaglia's basic theory is that love is learned and that everyone can and should learn to love.

Through his teaching, lectures and writings, Leo Buscaglia is exerting a timely influence on us all as he tells us what living is really all about.

ACKNOWLEDGMENTS

We are pleased to acknowledge permission to reprint brief quotations from the following works.

Carlos Castaneda, *The Teachings of Don Juan: A Yaqui Way of Knowledge*. Berkeley: University of California Press, 1968. The excerpt quoted from this book is reprinted by permission of The Regents of the University of California.

Alexandra David-Neel and Lama Yongdon, *The Secret Oral Teachings in Tibetan Buddhist Sects*. San Francisco: City Lights Books, 1967. Reprinted by permission of City Lights Books.

Charles Reich, *The Greening of America: How the Youth Revolution is Trying to Make America Livable*. New York: Random House, Inc., 1970.

Pitirim A. Sorokin, *The Ways and Power of Love*. Chicago: Henry Regnery Company, 1967.